SEE IT FROM MY SIDE

MY SIDE

A Father's Loss of His Daughter in the Opioid Crisis and the Dawn of Recovery

MARK TIMOTHY WEBB

ISBN: 9781070284095
Imprint: Independently published

Available from Amazon.com and other retail book outlets.

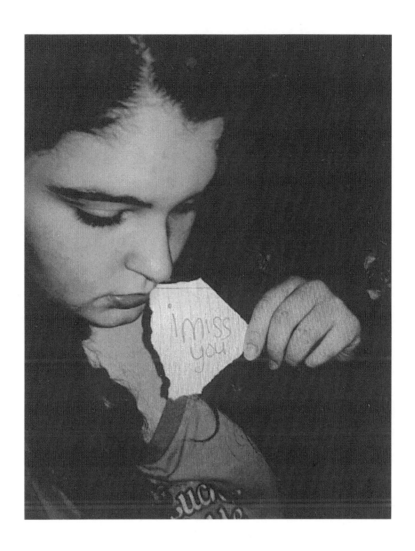

DEDICATION

In memory of my daughter,
Brooke Ashley Webb,

and dedicated to

My sons, Brandon and Cody, and my granddaughter,
Baylee. They lost their sister; she lost her world.

TABLE OF CONTENTS

ACKNOWLEDGMENTS

Maryville United Pentecostal Church
Your prayers kept me uplifted and going forward.

Celebrate Recovery
A wonderful place that truly saved my life.

Mrs. Jan McCoy
*My friend who introduced me to
the Celebrate Recovery experience.*

All officers serving with Blount County Sherriff,
Maryville City Police Department, and
Alcoa Police Department in Tennessee
*For doing an extremely difficult job while
maintaining dignity and professionalism.*

Chip Hatcher, my Brother from Another Mother
*For the invaluable help on this project and
being my true friend and advisor all these years.*

and

My Entire Family
For supporting me through all the rough times I have had.

Credits:

The Holy Bible KJV
The Celebrate Recovery Program
Alcoholics Anonymous 12 Step Program

FEED NOT THE DEMON

Feed not the demon living within;
let me once again be whole.
By myself, I must endure the torture of my soul.
Death would be relief for me, but not for those around.
Family I once held dear, are nowhere to be found.
I let them down; I turned against the very life they gave.
I need them now, to be back with them,
tis all I hope to have.
Their child still loves them from within,
but they no longer see,
The life I live, the hurt I feel, the struggle to be free.

Feed not the demon, living within,
for it has been hungry far too long.
Take the feeling I have inside,
come make me whole and strong.
The life I want is within my reach,
I yearn for it every hour.
I know I will make it eventually,
with the help of my Higher Power.
The scars on my arm, and those in my heart,
serve as reminders to me,
To do all I can to shed this hell, and regain my sanity.

Feed not the demon, shake free from it, and let it finally die.
Remove the hold it has on me,
it keeps me down no matter how I try.
My life has been turned upside down,
I don't know right from wrong.
Return to me the life I had,
full of happiness and song.

Feed not the demon, is a fight I face each and every day.
I walk alone, but try to help those struggling along the way.
Free I from my world of torment, my soul begins to cry.
Give me help to spread my wings, and let my spirit fly.

~ Tim Webb, April 2019

The inspiration of this poem comes from my baby girl. Most of her life, she and I were connected to same wave lengths. We knew each other's thought before speaking. She was a total "Daddy's girl," and we were very close. That is, until the end of her days. Although she loved me, I was ostracized from the Brooke I knew. I knew not the person she had become. Before addiction that consumed her life, she loved writing stories and poems and was quite good at it. Several songs she composed were worthy of being recorded, but unfortunately she didn't commit them to paper. I would love to have been able to see them recorded in her honor. Just like her, they are gone forever.

I never intended on writing a poem on the stated subject, or any subject for that matter. But my heart, mind, and hand had other intentions. As unaccustomed as I am to writing prose, I could not decide on what to pen. I sensed a strange, but familiar, feeling in my office while pondering. It was as if someone was in the room with me. I soon realized I felt my baby girl all around me and words began to flow. I truly feel this is what Brooke would have said if she had been able. I see her prints all over the page this poem was written on. I have let many people read it and give me their opinion. It has been said that it is very deep, and encapsulates the struggles of addiction very well. One person accused me of being an addict, because I could not know how to describe the pain this well. I am not an addict, and I simply wrote the words my heart was giving me.

For reasons beyond my comprehension, I wrote the poem, but I am unable to memorize it. I felt the touch of God in the writing, so I am positive this is intended to help many. I pray it touched you while reading it.

FOREWARD

I will never forget the afternoon of Wednesday, May 23, 2018. I was sitting on the sofa watching TV. There was a knock at my front door. As I arose from the sofa to go get the door, I could see through the door window that it was Tim. Now, this is a man I have known for a decade. We met as Boy Scout leaders and formed a Scout Troop. Then, we had been Freemasons together. We had done many, many things and been many, many places together over the years. I was closer to him than my own blood brother. We both knew each other's kids and family. We were brothers from another mother. Five days earlier, we had attended the funeral of one of our previous Boy Scouts, who had died of an apparent suicide. He was 19 years old, honors university student, outstanding musician, and this event had overwhelmingly stunned us all. I knew Tim had brought some news about it, as the death circumstances had not yet been disclosed by the family.

When I opened the door, Tim just stood there and I said, "Well, come on in"! As I turned and walked through the foyer, I noticed Tim had not moved. I turned back around and ask him what was wrong. I knew there was something wrong. He was not his normal, jovial self. He stepped in with a stoic face and said, "My baby girl passed away this

1

afternoon." It was the most solemn expression and tone I had ever seen on his face and heard him speak in. I said, "Oh no!", hugged him, and we sat down. He sat, still in shock from the deputy's previous informative visit, and explained to me what had happened earlier in the day.

How could this have happened to such a wonderful girl? I mean, I had known Brooke for years. She had been the babysitter for our daughter; the only one she ever had. Our daughter had (and still does have) posters hanging on her bedroom walls and door that she and Brooke had made over the years. Brooke played the piano at church every Sunday Morning. She had a beautiful baby girl herself. This couldn't be real. I knew it wasn't real...but...it was.

My wife and I knew that Brooke had been using drugs, but thought that she had stopped and was appearing to stay clean. We were both now very concerned about Tim. Tim was always the peacemaker. He was still in shock. I was not. Being an Army veteran and retired law enforcement, I was ready to go suit up and start tracking down drug dealers like a vigilante. The first several months were very hard on everybody. We had all experienced two deaths, back to back, of those dearest to us. I kept looking at a picture I had of the two great young people together, whose lives had ended way too early...almost simultaneously.

Eventually, Tim and I were talking about what all had happened and his experience in the process. Tim decided to put his story down on paper. He had been asked to speak a few days later at a local recovery group from the prospective of a parent's loss. He wrote out a 30-page testimonial speech for the event, which, in time, eventually became this book.

Being a published author, I offered to help him publish his story. By this time people were asking him to come to their groups and speak regularly, sharing his story. His story seemed to touch others in a special way like many did not. Tim's idea was to publish his story so that all those living and associated with this barbaric epidemic could read and understand the horrors that come with drug addiction, and often times, death as the resulting end factor.

This book tells Brooke's story through Tim's eyes. It tells the story of what Tim dealt with concerning his daughter, Brooke; what he had to deal with concerning himself; and, what you can expect to go through, if you are unfortunately trapped or drawn into this tragic situation.

It is a must read for every child, teenager, and adult who is considering, currently using or has experienced substance abuse or may be heading toward it. It is not just for the "user'" but for everyone and anyone whose lives have been directly touched by drugs or indirectly affected as a family member or friend. It is a story to be shared over and over again until everyone understands.

Let's stop the issue before it becomes an even more deadly problem than it already is. It's easy to say that, but we all have to take off the rose-colored glasses and do it by helping others that we know that can't do it on their own before it is too late. It is called Unconditional Love. That you are reading this means that you understand. The next step is to share this story, and your own story, with others.

Chip Hatcher
Friend & Brother of the Author

Brooke, you will always be remembered.

You will never be forgotten. We love you.

INTRODUCTION

This book is not a roadmap to recovery for anyone. Recovery and healing is partly due to what we read, hear, and do. I can read all day long, but until I put what I have read to work, it is simply words on a page. My prayers are that the words written here find their way into your heart and give you peace and comfort in dealing with the loss of your loved one.

The loss of a child does not mean the end of your life.

I know, first hand, it will feel like it, but trust me, you will get through this. People would tell me that, and I my reply to them would be they were crazy. I also told them I wasn't sure I wanted to get through it. I have also been told that time heals. The truth is that time aids in healing, but we will never heal completely. It is sad to think that thousands of parents have lost a child through the past years. It is even more heartbreaking to know that thousands of parents will lose a child in the years to come. Children are not the only ones suffering from this epidemic. People from all age brackets and all walks of life can be affected.

The peace and comfort that comes from God completely

overshadows anything man can give us. As much as we find ourselves needing others to talk with, we will find it is much more important to talk with God.

Matthew 5:4 says, "Blessed are they that mourn, for they shall be comforted."

The comfort that can only come from God will give us strength beyond measure. It is imperative that we stay strong. It is impossible to feel like we can, but it is important, just the same. Through the loss of a child, we will discover how weak we are, but through healing, we will find how strong we have become.

I am a father dealing with the loss of my precious daughter, Brooke Ashley Webb. I know there are other fathers feeling the exact hurt and loneliness as I have felt. I am not sure how many are willing to talk, because it is usually mothers who take the initiative of talking. God bless both fathers and mothers for the loss of a child. I have to be the voice for my daughter, as there is no other voice. Her mother is absent from the scene (also passed away from an overdose of drugs). Since, in reality, we will never have our child again, we must be strong and stand against what took them from us.

My name is Tim Webb, and I am the father of a late heroin addict daughter. The pages set before you are intended to express what I went through. As a father, I saw things the same as a mother would, but dealt with them from a different perspective. While taking nothing away from a grieving mother, it is my hope that people will see the difference and understand the father's point of view.

I have been lied to, stolen from, manipulated, cursed at, yet chose to overlook it all and see only what I wanted to see. What I wanted to see was the baby girl we brought home from the hospital in August 1992. But, that was not to be. I was the type of parent that would say, "Not my child, not my baby." I had to admit to myself, yes, it was my child, my baby. I had no idea how to help her, because she didn't want Daddy to know the depths of her addiction. This was a part of her world, and I was not invited to visit. She wanted me to be proud of her. I was proud of what she used to be, and not what she had become. I was so proud of my baby girl, but I didn't know the addict living in her body.

CHAPTER 1

Brooke Ashley Webb, born August 25, 1992, was pretty much the typical daughter. The kind of daughter with a little bit of an attitude. Did I say a little attitude? Oh no, I meant to say Brooke had a LOT of attitude. She was still my baby girl and totally owned my heart. I was so very proud of her. I reflect back to the day that Brooke's mother and I got our divorce. I often wonder if I had stayed in the marriage, would things have turned out better. But on the opposite side of the coin, we didn't stay together, and our children actually turned out better.

Brooke had two brothers. Brandon, her older brother is two years older, and Cody, her younger brother, is two years younger. Brooke was the middle child, and by the time she was three years old, it was evident she was the alpha child. All three children loved each other, but the boys knew Brooke was boss. Her brothers never questioned or resented the position she had acquired. They obeyed her commands to a fault. Of all three of my children, Brooke was the one I thought would never do anything like this.

Brooke's short story starts only 26 short years ago. She was born in Knoxville, Tennessee, and was the only granddaughter my parents had. She was something special from the very start. I knew she would one day do a great work for God. As time passed and Brooke grew into a fine young lady, she started developing stomach problems. We took her to the hospital several times and were eventually told she had a condition called Ulcerative Colitis. She was diagnosed at a hospital designed for children, and her doctor told us she would have problems her entire life.

Ulcerative Colitis is a chronic disease in the large intestine, in which the intestine and colon become swollen and causes small open sores, or ulcers. These sores develop pus and mucous. The disease also comes with some pain and discomfort. She also had female problems in which she endured quite a bit of pain from monthly cramps.

After our divorce, Brooke's mother found it easier to take her to the emergency room for treatment of her ailment. She quit making doctor appointments and stopped buying the prescribed medicine for treating Brooke's condition. I was carrying Brooke on my insurance plan through work, and I thought she was still visiting her doctor and getting the medicine through him. I was never told any difference. The emergency room would diagnose, but not treat the problem. The attending doctor would give her something to bring her pain under control until she could get to her doctor. Brooke always came home with a bottle of pain pills. This was, ultimately, the way her addiction began.

Things progressed over the next few years in this similar way, and then her mom decided to get into the pain pills. I am not a fortune teller by any stretch of the imagination. I remember when our children were young. I went to the doctor for persistent cough, was diagnosed with bronchitis, and was given a prescription for cough medicine with codeine in it.

Codeine is an opioid used for treating mild pain. I have no clue why it was prescribed to me, as I had absolutely no pain, just a persistent cough. I took it for one day and hated the way it made me feel. I was getting ready to pour it down the drain, when my wife, Teresa, asked me not to. Her exact comment was, "Hey, don't throw that away. Someone in the family may need it later." I didn't, and found the empty bottle the next day. She had taken the bottle and drank it much like one would drink a cup of coffee. I told her she would be a drug addict if she could afford it, and her response was, "yeah, probably."

Teresa began to notice Brooke's pain leave and how good the medicine made her feel. She decided to get in on it and developed ways to get pills for herself. She would always have some type back pain that warranted a trip to the emergency room. Teresa would get a bottle of pills for no other reason than to feel good. I am sure she had minor pains and aches, but nothing that justified her taking prescription pain medicine on a regular basis.

Eventually, when either of the two had the slightest pain, discomfort, or even an urge, they would go to the hospital and return home with a bottle of pain relievers. The pills they brought in would always be some type of opioid. Both Brooke and Teresa quickly became addicted. Soon, Brooke and Teresa were put on a list of suspected abusers from the hospitals they would visit. When the problem got so bad that neither could get anything stronger than an aspirin from any hospital, they remembered a friend Brooke had made in jail.

This person introduced them to stronger and cheaper alternatives. They were told they would have no pain, and experience a feeling unlike anything they have ever experienced. This was told to me my Brooke. One of the few times we actually talked about her alternative life. She kept the door locked to the rest of that life. I was never allowed to know anything else, and I didn't ask.

No person has ever gotten out of bed and decided they were going to become a drug addict. Addicts are made, not born. A child born with addiction problems was made an addict by the addicted mother, while in the womb. I have many friends who tell me they have an addictive personality and are afraid they could get addicted to anything, unless they are careful. One may want to be "cool," and just want to fit in with their friends.

So they try what their friends are doing. Or one may become an addict exactly how Brooke and her mother did; by getting hooked on prescription pain pills. Either way, once a person is hooked, there are only two ways out: either by getting into rehab to overcome the addiction and staying clean, or death.

With drugs, there is no "happy middle." This becomes the "all the way in, or all the way out" syndrome. The sad part is there are prescription pain medications available that are just as effective, and not opioids. Nor, are these alternative pills addictive.

It wasn't long before both of them were dabbling with liquid morphine. Brooke took it a step further and started experimenting with heroin. Oh, how my stomach turns, just saying that. I am not sure how long the addiction for either was, because they hid it from me very well. Several of her friends told me that she was into drugs, but I didn't want to hear that. I thought they were trying to make things up on her.

I once asked Brooke about the accusations, and she told me her friends were just mad at her and were trying to get her in trouble with me. She assured me there was no truth to their stories. I wish I had listened to them instead of Brooke. She hid it because she didn't want Daddy upset with his little angel. Her mom hid it from me, because she was afraid I would tell the police.

About a year and a half before she departed this earth, I discovered Brooke had been having some "run-ins" with the law. Since she wasn't working, she had to find a way to pay for her drugs. She got into shoplifting. Things seemed to go quite easily for her, until she got caught stealing some food for herself and her mother. She was subsequently arrested and taken to jail. This being her first offense, she was placed on probation, and she was ordered to take random drug tests. Everything went well, until she violated her probation for failing a drug screen. For failing, and violating, she was ordered to serve a 90-day sentence in the county jail.

After serving about 75 days, she was in court standing before the judge. He was very stern with her and told her she was going to be released. I was sitting in the room and remember hearing a word of warning he gave her that she was on a slow burn to a 2-year sentence. That didn't seem to bother her at all.

It is astounding and horrifying to witness how far drugs can take one from the path they were originally destined to travel. Drugs have a deadly schedule of their own. It is nearly impossible to disrupt that schedule. It can be done, with help and a lot of support. During the entire time she was locked up, I was an emotional wreck. I was emotionally strong enough to only see her twice, during her scheduled visiting hours. It broke my heart to see her in that god-awful striped suit and sitting behind a plexiglass partition.

She was released around 11:00 PM that night. I picked her up and brought her home. We talked and she told me she was going to straighten her act up. I was overjoyed that she was finally out and was going to get clean. I soon discovered that telling and doing are two different things. I thought that 75 days in jail would have been enough to help her start down the path to recovery, but found out that she was actually able to get high in jail. After she departed this life, I learned that 75 days is not nearly enough time to clean drugs out of an addict's system.

She told me that she had gotten high five or six times while in jail. She told me she made friends in there that were having morphine smuggled in. Brooke didn't comprehend that the reasoning of the person giving her the morphine was to keep her addiction alive. Her ulterior motive was to sell Brooke drugs after they both got out. She was careful not to tell me how morphine was brought in. After getting out, I am sure she resumed her shoplifting and stealing from other people.

I recently found out that every person I knew that had any contact with her was asked to loan her money. I am not sure if she did anything else to get money for her addiction. I really don't want to think of what else she might have done, but I have my suspicions. Shoplifting and stealing things from the house continued to transpire. During the first week after her mother's passing, her criminal activities increased, and she finally made the big time in the county beside where we lived.

As a result of feelings of guilt from her mother's death, she stole some rings from a lady that she and her mother cleaned house for. The rings were valued at over a thousand dollars each. She pawned them and got really messed up on drugs. Brooke had not developed into an intellectual criminal and was unaware that rings of such value have insurance policies on them. These policies are basically paper trails that follow a ring to wherever it ends up. They were found in a local pawn shop with her name on the receipt. She was subsequently arrested by officers in our county and held until officers from the neighboring county could pick her up.

So it went from simple shoplifting to two counts of felony theft. That 2-year sentence was beginning to look like a possible reality. But that didn't come close to stopping her.

An addict gets to the point where the need to get high outweighs the consequences of the action. The rational thinking part of the brain is taken over by the thought that getting high is more important than anything else in the world. Brooke didn't have to go to court for the felony charges, for she was gone before her date arrived.

CHAPTER 2

During the last year of Brooke's life, her actions were taking a toll on me. I was treated in ways that no father should have to deal with from his own child. I had musical instruments stolen and pawned, as well as many guns. She was taking things I bought for Baylee and exchanging them for money. I knew both Brooke and her mother were taking things, but they would never admit it.

At the time, I was unaware she was getting the money card out of my wallet and withdrawing small amounts of cash from my bank account. Some nights, I would go to bed with $60.00 cash in my wallet. The next day, when I opened it to pay for something I purchased, I would find only $20.00 inside. I once went to the grocery store to buy lunch items to take to work. I may have bought $30.00 worth of items and proceeded to check out. The wait to check out was not long, and I was soon at the register. After giving me the total, I opened my wallet to discover my cash and debit card were both gone. I left the store with nothing in hand.

I came home and found the debit card on my desk. (I never leave my debit card anywhere.) I asked Brooke about it and she had no clue how it got from my wallet to my desk. The cash I had in the wallet was gone, too, and once again, that was a total mystery to her. After that night, I kept my wallet in my locked truck with the keys in my pocket.

Brooke was stealing from me in ways that were hard to detect. She would take guns from my safe and move other guns around to void the empty spot. My guitar case would be exactly where I left it. I kept it slid under my bed to keep it from being in my way. The case would be exactly where I placed it, but the guitar would be gone.

She came up with stories like, "Oh, my friend wants to learn to play bass, and I took it over there to show her a few things. I just forgot to bring it home." After checking with her friend, and being told it was not there, I knew exactly where it was. I forced her to get it out of pawn and sold it the next day to keep her from pawning it again to get high.

Once, I received a call from the pastor of our church. The church's security camera caught Brooke and her mother stealing a guitar from the sanctuary. I found it at a local pawn shop and picked it up.

Things started disappearing from her grandmother's room. This was harder for us to detect, as her grandmother was older and getting forgetful. When I confronted her about things being gone, she would neither admit nor deny. The things she took from my mother held more sentimental valuable than what they were worth in cash.

One item I will never see again is my grandfather's wrist watch. He bought it when he was a young man, and gave it to me when I was 7 years old. The watch itself might have been worth a hundred dollars, but the sentimental value was priceless.

It was the coldness of her heart that I remember profoundly. Remorse was virtually non-existent in her life. I learned quickly to secure everything of value, even to the point of putting things in my safe or leaving them at friend's houses. It is a horrible feeling to know that a parent has to take measures to protect property from their own child. Such drastic methods caused me to feel I was a prisoner in my own home. I was so terrified to leave anything lying around. I came to the point where I was afraid to come home for fear of what would be missing next.

I would have sold everything I owned, if I knew it would have helped Brooke get, and stay, clean. As a father, I let things slide by and tried to convince myself that she was going to be alright. I now comprehend this was a dream. Brooke was never going to be alright. I never wanted her to steal from me, much less anyone else.

Brooke never wanted to be a thief, but the intense lust for that "high" turned her into someone that was no longer recognizable. Even a year after her passing, I still walk into pawn shops to look for deals and find things that were once owned, but never sold, by me.

From the beginning of their lives, I loved all three of my children unconditionally. Sure, I knew she was stealing from me, and yes, I did get very upset. But the love for my daughter was always without question. My sons are the same way. I have gotten disappointed with them at times over the years, but my love for them has never diminished. I know my children love me the same way.

Throughout their lives, I was not always there when they needed me, but their love for me was always strong. I had a job that required me to work long hours and many weekends. I think this is why I had such a problem admitting that Brooke was taking my things and selling them for drugs. I was completely heartbroken when I found my items in the pawn shop. It devastated me when I first realized she was stealing from me and using my debit card to deplete my checking account. But, my love for my daughter never faltered.

There is a major difference in unconditional love and trust.

She was my baby girl, my angel, my little gift from God, but she totally destroyed all the trust I had in her.

Things got so bad that whenever she was in the house, either my son or I always had her within sight. Going all the way back to my youth, I can remember having a problem with someone who either lied or stole. I never tolerated them then, and I don't tolerate them now. The same goes for my sons. If I find them to be stealing from or lying to me, my trust in them is gone. I will be done, but I will never stop loving them and would be the first one to help them any time of day or night.

My children are my world, and if I am wronged by one of them, my world does not crash down about me. Nothing will take away the love I have for my children. Trust and faith go hand in hand, and since my trust was broken with her, I had total faith that she would steal from me again. This was not a comfortable way for me to be with my daughter, but I had no choice.

Since her passing, I have been able to retrieve most of my property and most of the items I bought her. Fortunately for me, Brooke used one of two pawn shops I know quite well. I have friends working in both places and when I found any of my items for sale, I explained the reason it was in there. They were sympathetic and allowed me to pick it up at the same price it was originally pawned for. People have asked me why I buy her things back. They tell me it will only cause me to think of her more. I look them squarely in the eyes, and say "Exactly."

I will always wonder if I did the right thing by not turning her in to the police for stealing from me. I will never know the answer. I do know I did what I thought was right at the time. I also wonder if I would have had the courage to turn her in to the police. Would it have helped, or would it have destroyed her? To this day, I can't answer that question.

I have no idea how they could hide their disease as well as they did. I was around Brooke just about all the time, and she just appeared tired. When I asked her what was wrong, she would tell me that she was completely worn out. She was so convincing that I believed the lies she was telling me, but now I realize she was high. Since this was my first occasion of being around anyone high on drugs, I had no way of comparison with anyone.

I was awkwardly around Teresa quite often because Brooke and Baylee, my granddaughter, were living with me. She was at my house almost every other night, and I never noticed anything different about her.

About two months before her passing, and just before losing temporary custody of Baylee, Brooke had started moving her things into the house she and her fiancé were working on. They were planning on fixing the house up and moving their furniture in. When it was finished and ready to move into, they were going to be married.

Before addiction took over her precious life, we were at church every time the doors were open. Brooke played piano, and in addition, was an incredible singer. Her mother played drums, and I played bass guitar for her.

I observed tears flow down her face while she was playing. God would use her music to reach other people. I have seen her get up from the piano to go pray with or for someone. She would spend hours on end praying for people, and all the time, fighting the demon inside her. During the last year of Brooke's life, she got out of church, and I never saw her smile or laugh again.

It nearly destroyed me watching the internal fight going on within her. The hardest part was when I realized I could do absolutely nothing to help her.

The addict has to come to the point in life where they must decide they want help and ask for it. No one can make this decision for them.

For the first time in both her life and mine, Daddy was

unable to take the pain away from his child. I was unable to protect her from the evil working within her. Her pain was becoming my pain. I lived with this torment daily. What could I have done different? I have asked myself this on a daily basis. The only answer I discovered was: nothing.

I also remember asking myself, "Why my daughter?" I mean she grew up in church, and was mainly a wonderful girl. She was never into any mischief, before the drugs took over.

Romans 2:11, tells that "For there is no respect of persons with God."

When I read this, I realized it didn't matter if my daughter had been raised in church or not. It didn't matter if she was a great person or a horrible person. God shows no favoritism to anyone. Brooke was no better than anyone else.

After losing temporary custody of her daughter, and the dreadful thought of an impending prison sentence looming over her, Brooke finally hit "rock bottom." There was no way could she go except up. She told me she wanted help, and I enthusiastically worked with her to help find the help she desired. Phone calls were made by both of us, seeking help from an inpatient treatment center. She had no money, and therefore, no insurance.

With no insurance, the inpatient treatment center was an impossibility. She made an appointment with a local doctor to get a prescription for a medication called Suboxone®. This is a medication used to help take away the cravings of drugs, which helps addicts get clean of the drugs they are taking. She could not pay for the visit and the medicine, so her brothers and I did what we could. Everything we did for her was not enough.

Brooke would take some of the medication to relieve the craving of the drugs. She would break the pills into quarters which would be just enough to take the edge off. This was a mistake, because her demon was too strong. She would come off the medicine and get high, and them go right back on the Suboxone®. It was a total waste of money and effort for all concerned.

Now that I look back on the entire ordeal, I feel as if I had enabled Brooke. I was paying her car payment, her insurance, buying gas for her to run around, and giving her money simply to use to be able to go out with her daughter, Baylee. I did this all the while, knowing she was stealing from me. I am the kind of father that could not stand to see any of his children in need.

Unfortunately, I see now, this was the worst thing I could have done for her.

If you baby the addict, you will bury the addict.

I truly believe that she wanted to get clean and get her life in order to get her child back, but the demon inside her was stronger than the want of help. Although my sisters tried to help me through all this, I was pretty much alone. Brooke was alone in her addiction, and I was alone watching her.

CHAPTER 3

Brooke's journey ended on May 23, 2018, and my journey started the same day. It has been a very troubling trip. It was, still is, and will forever be, a journey I wish no parent would have to take. Unfortunately, until things change and laws are passed, (I am not going into politics, here) many of our children will overdose and die. Until enough light is shed on this situation, nothing will stop or even slow this problem. More effective laws and policies need to be developed to curtail the influx of drugs.

Few people know of programs designed to help addicts. Most are content, like I was, to keep their head in the sand about the entire situation. It is the "out of sight, out of mind" concept. The idea of "I don't think about it until I am forced to think about it" rationale is wrong. When we are forced to think about it, then it has already hit home, and it is too late to think about it. It then becomes time to do something about it. It is becoming impossible to keep from knowing someone, or a family of someone, who has not been visited by the angel of death from a drug overdose.

On Wednesday, May 23, 2018, two Blount County Sheriff deputies knocked on my door. This had become quite the norm for me. Usually, they were picking Brooke up or serving some type of papers. This time was very different. The mood was very somber, and I knew, almost immediately that something was wrong. They asked if my daughter had a drug problem, and I told them, yes, she did. My world crashed before me at their next statement.

One of the officers, (one of whom I had spoken with 6 months previous concerning Teresa), informed me that Brooke, my baby girl, my angel, had passed away from a heroin/fentanyl overdose. Actually, it was not the heroin that took my baby away, it was the fentanyl in it. I have discovered that a dose of fentanyl the size of 2 grains of sand is enough to kill a person. The fentanyl level in her blood was quite heavy, which means she had much more than what was needed...more than a lethal dose.

I was totally numb. I knew I really didn't hear them right. I knew they had me confused with another Tim Webb. No, I was the right Tim, and Brooke was the right Brooke. I died that day with my daughter, but I was the one forced to stay here and keep going. I was a living creature in a dead man's body. I sat there for what seemed like an eternity staring at the floor. I started sensing every emotion known to man.

Being the father of an addict is tormenting to say the least. Being the father of an addict who had just lost her mother to an overdose is one of life's most merciless tortures.

On Thanksgiving morning, November 23, 2017, her mother, Teresa, passed away from an overdose of prescription pain pills and a large amount of morphine. Along with the anguish of dealing with her own addiction, I saw the fresh grief in Brooke's eyes from losing her mother.

I saw the guilt she displayed in thinking her mom's death was somehow her fault. My son, Cody, later told me that Brooke was the person responsible for giving her mother the injection of morphine that ended her life. I have heard that addicts will "shoot up" with someone, but when they overdose, they are found totally alone. No one knows anything, and no one saw anything. Being lied to as much as I was, I must say I have no idea which one of them got into hard drugs first. It really doesn't matter anymore, because both are gone, and nothing will change that.

Thanksgiving morning of 2017, I was sitting on my couch totally oblivious to the world outside my door. I heard an ambulance racing down the road in front of my house, and thought to myself, "man, what a bad day for anyone to have to go to the hospital." Little did I know at the time, it was an ambulance speeding to where Teresa had overdosed and passed away. I was stunned and totally shocked at the news. I was married to the lady for almost 17 years and had no clue how to help my children.

I have witnessed death from a distance, but this was the first time it has trespassed into my life. The pain I felt from her death came from watching my children cope with losing their mom. Brooke left the house when her mom overdosed and called me within a few minutes. The lady, with whom Teresa had been staying, called the ambulance, while Brooke jumped into her car and left the scene. She told me they were taking her to the hospital and she was on her way there.

By the time I got there, my youngest son, Cody, was already there with Brooke, while my oldest son, Brandon, was at work. The hospital had placed Brooke and Cody in a small conference room by themselves. When I walked in, Cody told me, "Mom's gone." I left to pick Brandon up from work, and until then, it was the hardest scenario I have faced; to tell my son his mother had passed away from an overdose. Little did I comprehend that the actual hardest scenario was soon to be approaching on my horizon.

When Brandon and I arrived, we were ushered into the same room as Brooke and Cody. Within a few minutes, two detectives came in and began asking questions about Teresa. I let the kids answer the inquiries, because until then, I had absolutely no knowledge of Teresa using drugs.

I had knowledge of Brooke, but Teresa kept her usage confidential, and she always talked of wishing Brooke would get some help to quit. She was never high when I was around her. Now that I am looking back, maybe she was. Various times, I would come home from work and she would be lying on the couch asleep. I just thought she was tired. From what, I had no idea. This was similar to Brooke telling me she was always tired.

When they finished asking the kids things about their mom, one of the officers asked me to step outside because they needed to ask a few more questions of me. I obliged and was questioned about the possibility of her being an addict. I told them about the incident with the cough syrup, but I clarified that it was years earlier. I was told if she drank the cough syrup like that then, it would be nothing for her to do things now.

I told them she was staying with a woman Brooke had met while in jail. We discussed the possibility of the woman being a user, and according to Brooke, she was. She introduced me to this woman several months previous, and told me she was a user, but was working to get clean. I knew nothing else to tell them. They said that was enough information, and they told me they knew the woman Teresa was staying with.

I was told the woman had never attempted to get clean and was probably the source of drugs for her. They proceeded to tell me about items surrounding Teresa at the scene. They found a needle beside her, and the condition she was in was indicative of an overdose.

Their photographer took photos showing "track marks" on her arm. As much as I was around her, I never noticed any marks, because where they were, she kept covered. It was not until that very moment I realized the marks on Teresa, and the marks on Brooke were in the exact same place, on the inside of their arms and just below the elbow.

Since then, I have discovered addicts will "shoot up"

anywhere they can find a good vein. When one vein collapses, they will find another place. They also use inconspicuous places to avoid having the tell-tale track marks of using. I have heard of people injecting around genitalia, between fingers and toes, and even under the nails. Just because a person has no marks, fresh or old, on their arm, don't think they are "clean."

Even through all the grief and guilt Brooke was dealing with, it was not enough to take away the desire to get that next "high." I wanted to help her, but had no idea how to do it. In reality, the feelings I had were split between helping her and knocking her to the ground, hoping that would shake some sense into her. The latter, I knew, would do no good and would have only ended up with me going to jail. I saw the pain, suffering, and emotional stress on her young body that I could not take away.

While looking at the face of my daughter, I saw the face of the addict. I talked with my daughter, while talking to the addict. My daughter listened to my voice and heard my pleas to get help. The addict heard my voice, yet laughed in my face.

The hardness of addiction takes over all conscience.

It is hard to differentiate hating the addict while loving the child, when both share the same body. I love my daughter as much today as I loved her then. I totally hate the disease that took her away from me.

Drug addiction affects more than the addict. The choices made by the addict affect family and friends, people that are being stolen from, doctors, police and the entire court system. All family members and friends are reluctantly pulled into the world of lies and deceit. Every addict is someone's son or daughter, and each has at least one person wanting them to seek help. Every addict deserves the opportunity to be offered help, regardless of accepting or declining.

The entire financial burden of taking care of their mom's final expenses fell upon my children, as she had no money and no insurance to take care of her. My sister helped set up an online donation site, where money could be sent and used to take care of the final expenses. Family members were sending money to the kids for their mother's final expenses. Both my sons, Brandon and Cody, were receiving money and saving it for their mother.

Brooke was receiving money to help, but seemed to always "loose it," or someone got it out of her car or purse. She even came up with a story of letting her aunt (her mother's sister) hold the money, which she used it to pay her own bills. I thought she was telling the truth. She had become quite the accomplished liar. Her brothers became so incredibly angry that she had lost the money. They became upset beyond comprehension when they realized she was using it to feed her demon. Their anger toward her didn't upset her in the least. She was only concerned about that next high.

Brooke passed away completely alone in the confines of her house and alone in her addiction. Police ordered an autopsy to be performed. The official report was what we all knew it would be: an overdose. After two weeks, the body of my baby was released and delivered to a local funeral home, where arrangements were already in place.

Brooke visited me the night before she entered eternity, and I never gazed upon her sweet face again. She told me she just wanted to visit with me for a while. I am not sure if she just wanted to visit or wanted to try to pick something up to sell. Her memorial service was held as she was being taken care of. There was no body, no casket, no hearse, and only pictures of a once lively, beautiful girl. I walked into the church sanctuary and had to do an about face. I was not ready for what I was being forced to deal with.

I gathered all the mental strength I could muster, closed my eyes, and walked in. I saw the photo display my sisters had so lovingly assembled. I saw mementos of her short life displayed. I felt as though I had died there and no one noticed. I was surrounded by over 200 people, all telling me how they loved Brooke. Even then, I felt an overwhelming feeling of being totally alone, such as I have never experienced before or since. I was there in bodily form, but mentally shut off from the entire world. That very moment in time, it was just me and my dead daughter. Nothing else mattered and no one cared.

Just like Teresa, Brooke had no money or stable job, which hindered her from making progress in getting the help she needed. She had totally lost all interest concerning responsibility for her health, her situation, and even her daughter. In her unstable condition she would not have held onto a job very long. As a result of not working, she had no insurance for her final expenses.

We had no alternative other than having her cremated. Since I was in the process of paying her fines, car payments, insurance, and other things, I was not in the position to pay another $12,000 to bury her. I wish I could have paid it, but I still had my bills to worry about. Her ashes are with my sister, and I have not been able to see them. I even have the coroner's report in my file cabinet. It is in a large envelope and has not been opened by me, yet. I may be able to get to the point in my life, to be able to look at these items, but it will not be in the near future.

While helping with Brooke's belongings, my sisters discovered some personal letters she had written to me. She kept a journal in which she wrote daily, and she stated that she wanted to write each member of the family a letter, but the only letters she wrote were to me.

My sister, Bonny, told me the last letter addressed to me, started out by saying, "I don't know why I am writing this letter, and not sure when you will read it, but God knows." Bonny read bits and pieces to me, until I could handle no more and asked her to stop. The letter told of how much she loved me and how I was always there for her. I was her rock, and her safety. That was about all I could hear at the time, and have not attempted to read them yet. I feel as though Brooke had some type premonition of something happening to her. This is hard to explain, since I have no real proof.

I think she knew since becoming a drug addict that her time was limited. It is hard to understand her statement of my being her rock and her safety, since she was unable to talk with me about her addiction. She was an addict and was ashamed of her lifestyle. I would have helped get her the help she desperately needed. I would have been beside her every step of the way. I would have given my very life to help her regain hers.

I have heard that addiction is not a disease. I have heard the same thing about alcohol. I beg to differ here, but addiction and alcoholism ARE diseases. Cancer is a disease, and usually starts by introducing something foreign into body. Smoking cigarettes can cause lung cancer. Heart diseases are caused by introducing chemicals and fats into the body.

Pretty much every disease is introduced into the body from substances outside the body.

Becoming a drug addict is not a death sentence. Not seeking help to overcome addiction is. Just like other diseases, precautions must be taken to prevent relapse and the disease returning. There are an inconceivable number of people who have overcome addiction. One may take medications to keep disease dormant. Addiction is the same.

The life of a grieving parent is full of "what if's." What if I had found this out earlier? What if I had I had forced her to get help? What if I had reported her stealing to the police? Don't beat yourself up over these questions. Many are the times I have wondered if Brooke would still be here if I had reported her for stealing guns. She still would not be home, but would have been in jail, maybe getting help for her problem.

What if I had forced her into some type of in-patient rehab center? Then, I wonder if she would even speak to me when she got out. This type questioning can go on forever. It is enough to drive one insane. I am not a proponent in the theory of predestination; hence, I believe that whatever happened, happened for a reason. There is no alternative way it could have gone.

CHAPTER 4

Nothing a parent can do will make any difference. Until the addict is ready for help themselves, they will never be willing to change. We can't make their decisions for them. Brooke once told me that I was the very reason she overdosed on a few occasions. (Yes, she overdosed many more times than once.) She put the blame on me in front of a police officer and an EMT who were working with her.

At this precise moment, I looked into the eyes of my daughter and realized I no longer knew the eyes that were glaring back at me. I no longer knew the drug addict standing before me. The officer looked at her, then faced me and told me that was a bunch of crap. He proceeded to tell me she was going to get high, and was just looking for a reason and someone to blame.

The choice was made when our child became an addict. Even when someone becomes an addict, he, or she, is still responsible for their actions. For the first time in my life, I knew what it was like to hate the addict with hatred beyond description. I watched the people working with Brooke, trying to save her life. I sat in the corner of her bedroom, holding my 4-year-old granddaughter as she was crying and begging the police officer, "Please don't take my mommy to jail." The tears in Baylee's eyes were met with an icy cold stare from her mother. At that precise moment, I realized my daughter was lost somewhere in her own body and was being governed by the addict.

After the loss of my baby, I have given the same advice to every parent I come in contact with, "Please, be the child's parent and not their friend." Parents are given a responsibility over their children, to raise and train them the way they should go.

The time in life for a parent to become their child's friend, is after their child has children of their own.

It does not work if one parent is the parent, while the other is the friend. I was the parent, and I was the one that was made to look bad to my child. I love my children and tried to correct each of them, from their early years through their teens. I looked especially bad when I would try to correct Brooke, and her mother would take her side.

Brooke lived with me until she was 16 and moved back in with Teresa where she was told things like, "It is alright, go ahead and do what you want." She was even told, "Even though he is your father, you live with me and don't have to listen to him." Great way to talk to a child, isn't it? In my heart, I believe Brooke saw through her mother's attempt to sway her intentions and do what Teresa wanted to do.

I think she remembered who was with her during the important times of her life, but she didn't want to make waves and upset her mother. Her mother had a way of making Brooke and her brothers feel very guilty, if they upset her or did anything to cross her.

She wanted to be Brooke's friend, and would actually get mad at her for visiting friends without allowing her to tag along. As a result of trying to "fit" in with Brooke's friends, her mother, Teresa, got into opioids, too. It started the same way as Brooke. She saw the way the medicine took away the pain and wanted to get in on the action.

I read something once that said that God only loans people to us to help fulfill our lives. Treat them well, because one day, He will want them back. I believe both the mother and father will be held responsible for how a child is raised. It takes two to make a baby, and takes two to raise a baby.

Take care of the child God has placed in your keeping.

The father's aspect of the loss of an addict child is somewhat different than the mother's. Mothers usually have a network of close friends, or can find a support group. God bless mothers for the suffering they endure, and yet be strong enough to support the helping of others. I can't fathom the heartache of seeing a child leave this world, after carrying it for 9 months and giving birth to it. We fathers tend to be more the type to be tough and try to handle things on our own. The more I showed I could handle this by myself, the more I realized I couldn't.

Everyday rituals were absent from my mind. I didn't realize I needed a shower until my son told me. He said, "Dad, you haven't had a shower in almost a week. Don't you think it is time, because you are starting to smell ripe?" What an embarrassing statement to hear from my son. I know he really didn't want to say this to me, but did it because he loved me.

I thought I had taken a shower yesterday, and then noticed my yesterday was five days ago. Time seemed to stand still for me, yet, move quicker than normal. I was unaware that my life felt as if it was running twice the normal speed, yet actions around me were being seen in slow motion. I soon found that I was unable to trust my mental faculties, because part of my mind was closed down.

As a parent, I discovered pain at a new level. I felt emotional pain, as well as physical pain. The physical pain of aching to put my arms around my baby, holding her hand, feeing her touch upon my arm, was very real, very strong and very deep. I remember the pain in my chest from looking at a picture of us, taken a few days before she went home. The emotional pain is struggling through my day-to-day life. I know my daughter is now just a memory, but I was the dad, so I attempted to assure myself I could get through this myself. This is what I thought.

Fathers tend to be the strong supportive kind. We want to prove to the world that we need nothing or no one to help in any circumstance. We do not want to appear as weak to anyone, much less our family. We men, as a whole, are far less verbal, and try to handle any situation on our own, as we don't want people knowing our business.

We are, supposedly, the stronger of the two sexes (I apologize to any mother taking offense to this statement), and therefore able to handle more pain and stress. I have always had difficulty in saying I was unable to complete a project without help, and even not being strong enough. I have never asked anyone for help of any kind. I was not about to start asking now.

I feel the way I tried to handle losing my child may have caused me to become more feeble and unable to cope. Since May 2018, I have found out just how weak I truly am. After losing my child, I not only had to deal with the grief, but I had to deal with the feelings of being a total failure to her. I have two sons that I have to protect and not be a failure in their eyes.

I don't care how old a child is, I feel that a father will worry over the need to protect and provide for that child. If a father feels he can deal with it on his own, he is totally wrong. As a father, I had to swallow my pride and admit that I had become a total basket case and needed someone to talk with. I didn't see the need at first, but it became obvious to me quickly.

I had my job, had my work buddies, hunting friends, and I thought they would all help me get through this. But just like Brooke's addiction, this was a journey I took alone. My friends had no idea what to say or how to help. They tried, they failed. Not saying anything against any of them, but they have never walked this path. Unless a parent has lost a child, he or she will never understand the lingering emptiness and unfathomable longing. It is nothing like losing any other family member.

About a month before losing Brooke, a friend of mine lost his son. I tried calling him a few times but to no avail. I would send him a text giving my condolences, and he would text back, but no phone conversations. He was not ready to hear me, because I had not walked in his shoes. I had no idea the degree of suffering he was enduring.

The day after I lost my baby, I texted him to let him know I knew the feelings he was struggling with. I told him about losing Brooke, and within minutes, we were on the phone talking. We have talked quite regularly since. We talk because we can relate.

One difference between my friend and me is that I joined a group to help get through this, and he is still trying to deal with it on his own. He is doing better, but it is taking longer to cope. I pray for my friend daily. I lost my father in 1992, and I still miss him and would love to see him. But, the longing I have to see and hold my daughter is unsurpassed. It will be the same for the ones of us who are grieving for a lost child.

More than once, I have heard of parents splitting and divorcing over the loss of a child. I feel it is because mothers and fathers grieve and handle the loss in totally opposite manners. Communication declines in situations such as these. Many marriages could possibly be saved if better communication existed between them at this crucial time. Actually, marriages could be spared the agony of divorce if better communication existed between couples.

Support groups are a necessity for both parents, and in many cases, even the siblings. Parents may find it beneficial to sit in different groups, away from each other. Once they have begun the healing process, they may want to continue in a group together. Brooke's two brothers handled her passing in completely opposite behaviors. Brandon, her older brother, got mad at her for putting the family through all she did while using.

His feelings of anger have continued beyond her passing. He has held it all inside. I worry about him terribly. It is never a good thing to hold such emotions in. We must all find a "relief valve" of some type to vent our frustrations. Cody, her younger brother, was closer to Brooke. He cried and mourned in a way that only a brother could. I have tried talking to them about some type of support group and have gotten nowhere with either.

I was the father that thought I could get through on my own. I have always been the kind of man that hated depending on anyone for help. Why should this be any different? This choice of thinking almost cost me my very life. Not long after Brooke left, my sister called me. She told me one of her friends had lost a son to drugs. Her friend asked if she could call me. I said yes, and within an hour, we were talking.

I thought I was dealing with something no one else had ever experienced before. Although I felt a sense of comfort in meeting someone dealing with the same issue as me, I also experienced a feeling of sorrow. For it is the pain and suffering they are going through, I know all too well. It was difficult for me to hear, "You will get through this." Deep down, I knew I would, but I just couldn't see it. In recent meetings, I have let parents know they would get through it, just like I am.

Recently, I spoke with a lady who lost her son. I saw the rawness of the grief in her expression, and the disbelief that shown all over her face. I assured her she would get through it. She looked at me strangely when I quietly told her, "You will smile again."

I strongly advise any parent grieving from the loss of a

child to get into some type of support group as soon as possible.

As important as a support group is, having God in your heart is a necessity. God gives us peace and comfort at all times.

The healing process will actually start while taking part of the group. In the beginning, the pain I felt was quickly turning into anger. I realized that I was becoming a very bitter man. The anger was only seconded by hatred.

After joining and working with a support group, I have let the anger subside and replaced the hatred with love and a strong desire to help others. I have found myself becoming passionate in wanting to help others who are hurting and struggling. Although my passion and concern grows for the struggling, the anger and hatred for drugs continues to abide within me. This same group of people I didn't know a year ago has become my new family. My actual family is there for me, and always will be, but there is something special in the feelings I get when working with my group family. I never want to find myself without them.

As a father, I spent my life working to provide for my family. I endeavored to give my children a better life than I had. What parent does not want this? I did without so they could have. Many hours of overtime were worked for the betterment of my family. It was difficult to divide myself between my job and my family, but I did my best.

In the past, I have apologized to all of my children for not being there sometimes when they needed me. They have all told me everything was alright. They knew I loved them, and they understood. They told me I was a great father and they loved me. I often wonder how this "great father" didn't pick up on subtle signals from my daughter.

CHAPTER 5

I have always tried to make each holiday a special event around the house. We did the July fireworks, Memorial Day trips, Easter traditions of gathering with the entire family. Every holiday has become difficult to endure, but the first Thanksgiving was extremely testing.

About two weeks before the first Thanksgiving without her, I did an interview with a local television station entitled, "An Empty Chair at the Holiday Table." I spoke of the place where my daughter sat beside me. It would be set for her, but would be an unoccupied space. That may sound crazy, but I did it to honor her memory.

The mood around the table was subdued, as we ate our dinner in silence. The jovial aura was completely dismissed and everyone seemed to be resigned to maintain composure. My granddaughter, Baylee, made Thanksgiving easier to bear for us all. But the void was there and will be there forever.

Christmas was even harder for me. Along with Brooke's help, I was always the one putting Baylee's toys together. This year, I put them together, alone. The tradition of me, Brooke, and Baylee decorating the tree, was a thing of the past. I decorated it by myself. My heart was not in it, and I almost took it down when I discovered the handmade ornaments Brooke had made from Christmas' past.

The lights were especially beautiful this time. They were shining brightly and looked as though they were surrounded by a misty haze. I looked around the living room and everything had the same haze. It was then I realized I was looking around through tear filled eyes.

I was Santa by myself, and I watched the amazement of Christmas come alive in a 5-year-old's eyes. My baby should have been here to watch her baby open the presents Santa brought. The joy and laughter that Baylee displayed served to give me a sense of being. That baby put a smile on my face that would have made her mommy so happy. As much as I tried to provide a good Christmas for my sons and granddaughter, the emptiness within me was almost overwhelming.

I smiled and laughed with my family as best I could, but a large part of me was missing and will be gone forever. The smiles and laughter were a facade, used only to hide the depth of pain I was feeling. It didn't work, as my family saw the loneness in my eyes and the meaningless expressions on my face. I know their intentions were well meant, but they never left my side or let me be alone. I appreciated their attentiveness, but I wanted to be alone.

Buying the presents was difficult for me. While I was married to my children's mom, I was always the one to buy things for them. She never wanted to be involved. Her, "I trust you to buy the right presents," let me know she really had no idea what to get them. I did the best I could, and always seemed to put smiles on their faces. This year, like all the others, fell on me to buy everything. But this year, I had one less person to buy for. I had a cart full of items bought for my family. But the excitement and enthusiasm was not there, as I knew I had bought nothing for my daughter who had just become a memory.

Birthdays are also a battle for me to deal with. Brooke left this world three months and two days before her 26th birthday. That day was a distortion to me, as I was still reeling from the initial shock of losing her. Although I had three months to prepare for this one day, it made no difference. The significance of the day only served to intensify my pain.

I woke that morning, and grabbed the phone to call her. I decided to text her instead, and then realized neither would be necessary. I have no daughter to wish Happy Birthday. I will never again be able to take her out for her birthday dinner. No more cards will be bought for her. I will celebrate her birthday alone, longing just to hold her and talk with her once again. On the other hand, I will never celebrate my birthday with her again. That card I would get from Brooke will never appear. No more phone calls of "Happy Birthday, Daddy. I love you and hope your day is a good one."

There is a pain created from the brain and spinal cord, called "phantom pain." People sometimes feel this pain from a limb or appendage they have lost. I can still feel my arms around her holding her and running my hands through her hair. I have held her tight every day since she has been gone. I can actually feel her in my arms, just like a phantom pain. I will continue to hear her singing in my heart until my dying breath. Then, I will see her and hear her sing again. I await the day when I can actually sing with her.

Baylee is beginning to sing with songs from her favorite cartoon shows, and she sounds just like Brooke did at her age. She has discovered how to make short videos on my phone and her tablet. She made several of her singing to the television. It reminds me so much of things Brooke would do.

She wants to play piano like her mom, and I have promised to get her lessons when she is a little older. She is so impatient, as her mother was at that age, but if I remember correctly, most every 5-year-old is impatient. She has a difficult time talking about her mom, which is understandable. I look at her and I see the daughter I knew, looking back at me through the eyes of her daughter. When I hug Baylee, I feel so close to Brooke.

This precious child has seen more death and heartache than any child of five should ever see. She saw her grandmother dead on the floor of a bathroom where she had overdosed. She was taken from her mother and put in custody of her father and forced to live in a home with people she barely knew. She witnessed her mother overdose on several occasions and had to deal with her death too.

The final memory I have of Brooke and me talking will be stored in my mind for the rest of my days. It happened the night before she passed. I remember fondly, Brooke and I were having a conversation on cell phones. We were not actually talking but were texting each other. The discussion was the usual talk. Her asking me for money, and me telling her I had none.

Truth is, I did have money, but I was not going to give it to her to get a fix of heroin. I think, deep in her heart, she knew I had the money and knew the reasoning behind my telling her I didn't. I had gotten to the point that I could not endure the agony of helping her get her next fix. The part I remember most is that the conversation ended on an up note. She told me. "That's ok, Daddy. Have a good night, I love you, and I will see you tomorrow." I told her that I loved her. Those were the last words we shared.

That tomorrow never happened. It is heart wrenching to think of people who have departed this earth with someone mad at them. The words, "I am sorry, and I love you," will never be spoken again. "Please forgive me," will resonate in minds always. Words of anger or hatred will be endlessly remembered by the one speaking them. There will never be a chance for apologies to be uttered. My grandmother used to say, "Don't go to bed angry at anyone, because you never know if you will see them again." She was so right.

Something I regret doing is deleting all the text messages between Brooke and me. I had no clue her last message would be the last one I would get. I would have saved it and cherished it. Neither of us knew we would not speak again. Take care of the memories you have and take care of the little things, like text messages, small notes, or anything else between your child and you. It may very well be the last thing you share.

The "club" we now belong to, which I call the "Club of the Grieving Parent," is not an exclusive club. It is, unfortunately, open to all parents from generations past to generations future. It does not worry about financial standings, race, origin, or religious affiliations. In this club, there are no leaders or officers. Each member is on an equal level. It is also a club I wish no parent was ever involuntary allowed to join, because the dues are extremely too expensive. It is sad to believe that new members are joining every day, and at an alarming rate.

Drug addiction is not the only way for a parent to become a member of this club. One may lose a child in a vehicle wreck, suicide, and many other ways. I don't want to dwell on these methods for membership.

Upon becoming a member, we become a separate group from all other parents. We will never have the opportunity to be thrown out or withdraw our membership. On becoming a member, we take the obligation that we are members for life. Non-members will never understand the pain and emotions we are dealing with.

I am a father of three children, who has lost one child. That does not relieve me of my duties to my sons. I still have to be "Dad" to them when they need me. Brooke had several friends that considered me as "Dad" to them. Not only have I had to console my sons, I have had to comfort my other "children." There was one girl at Brooke's memorial service that just collapsed into my chest. She was one of Brooke's best friends. They grew up together and loved each other as actual sisters would.

I have called this precious girl my other daughter, because she and Brooke were inseparable since they were very young and in church together. They truly acted like sisters because where one of them was, the other was very nearby. They always had each other's back. She sends me several messages a week, telling me she loves me and is thinking about me. Messages of encouragement were sent back to her, along with prayer.

I have many of Brooke's friends contacting me, just to say hello. It might be a simple text message of "Hi Pops, just thinking about you," to a lengthy letter.

Many of her friends, some of whom I have never met before, continue to maintain an open line of communication with me. I love all my other children. It matters not the size of the message. It is wonderful to know after a year, Brooke is still missed by them, and they take time to say hello to me. It is amazing how much my girl was loved. As much as their calls and messages comfort and sooth my aching heart, I check on them and send them uplifting words, as often.

Going back to church was very difficult for me. It might be for you as well, but it is something we need to do. I never quit going, but more like took some time off. The worst part for me was going in and seeing the empty pew where Brooke would sit. I couldn't pay attention to the preaching for longing to see her sitting there again.

As I mentioned earlier, she played piano while I played bass guitar. I have long since resumed my position, but find myself almost unable to play songs I remember playing with her. I struggle to hold back my tears as I play, and do the best I can. I, however, find a strange sense of peace in playing the songs we played and soon realize the peace I am feeling comes from God. I can still hear the way she played and hear her voice singing the songs that are still being played. In my mind, I still see her sitting on the pew where we always sat. I will have a difficult time with this for the rest of my life. As difficult as it was, getting back into church was what I needed more than anything else.

CHAPTER 6

Although the grieving process will be similar for everyone, it will be unique to each. It will be a passage that we will take on our own, and every person will come out with different scars. Even husbands and wives will grieve in a similar way, but totally different. It is a well-traveled road that we will all take, in our own way and in our own time.

There are several stages of the grieving process. We will take each one step at a time.

1. Shock and Denial

The initial shock of finding that a child has been lost to a drug overdose, or for any other matter, is such that we will never forget. It is the kind of shock that will remain alive in our hearts forever. I felt like I had my breath knocked out by a speeding bus. I kept telling myself that it was not my child, not my baby, but it was.

As I mentioned earlier, when the officers told me what happened, I felt as though my soul and body separated for a moment. I motionlessly sat on my couch and stared at the floor as they explained what exactly went on at the scene. I heard words, but I could not acknowledge them. I saw the officers, and for a moment, I had no clue who they were. I could feel their presence, but couldn't distinguish them. I tried to talk, but nothing came forth except some guttural sound. I could not raise my arms nor move my legs. My heart felt as if it was going to explode.

Clearly, these officers had witnessed everything I was going through at that precise moment, while preforming their duties with others. They were very sympathetic and compassionate during the entire time they were talking with me. I do remember at one point, their asking me if I was alright. I turned my head and looked at them. I forced myself to tell them I was okay, because one had his radio out and was calling an ambulance for me. Their professionalism was most reassuring. These wonderful people have a very difficult job to do, and I thank them for the courtesy shown to my family and me.

Early on, right after learning about Brooke, I remember having a difficult time trying to sleep. I am a man who is not afraid of anything, but when I would lie down to go to sleep, I would be totally petrified with fear. I was afraid of the dark, and of being by myself. I knew nothing was there, but I was terrified of everything. I remember lying in bed and trembling with dread. It was awful to be this way, but I couldn't help it.

Even with it being the month of May, I remember myself freezing so bad; I thought I was going to have to put my coat on. I could not get comfortable anywhere I was. I always seemed to have a sense of urgency to be somewhere else, no matter where I was. I remember having no appetite at all. I know that experiences vary from one person to another, but I am willing to bet that others have felt, or are going through, what I have described. The body does strange things when dealing with shock.

Grief comes in waves. Some of the waves are little ripples, while others come in as tsunamis. We may think we are getting over it, and then something triggers the emotion again. It might be something as simple as hearing a song, the scent of an aroma, or seeing a road sign she commented on.

Anything can trigger grief. Be prepared to be hit with it at the most inopportune time. I know I have been hit several times. I have returned to playing bass at church, and songs that Brooke played sometimes would be chosen to play. It doesn't matter who is playing the piano or singing, I still hear my baby. Grief reminds me that I have a wound that will never heal completely. At best, the wound will cease to be visible, but will still be there.

Denial is a part in which I have spent a lot of time. My thoughts were very imaginable for me to believe, but absurd to actually think they were true. I remember thinking to myself that Brooke is really not gone. I had convinced myself that she was hiding in some witness protection plan, because the police promised to help her get "clean" if she would talk about her dealer. I could see her in a motel somewhere, wondering what we were going though. I actually felt the wrong numbers I frequently got on my phone were actually her just wanting to hear my voice. I mean, this is all possible, isn't it? I would try to rationalize this, and one day, when the dealer was put away, Brooke would come back home. Everything would be alright, and my family would all be together again.

I can't count the times I caught glimpses of her in grocery stores, restaurants, or gas stations. I seemed to see her everywhere I would be. My baby was alive somewhere and waiting for things to work out, and then she was coming home. I had myself totally convinced into believing my imagination.

Two nights after her passing I was online looking around, and got a notice that she was online in a social media sight. I became so excited I could hardly sit still. I knew then that she was alive. I could hardly contain the exhilaration I felt, until I remembered the police had her phone and had it turned on for their investigation. All hopes and dreams I had were dashed in a moment.

I carried this idea for quite a while, until one day realized it was a facade. Brooke is truly gone, forever. Even though I now realize this, I still find myself waiting on her to walk through the front door of the house. This may not be as much denial but more of a longing to see her again. I know that I will, one day, see her again. Not in this life, but in the next. Denial was thriving while I was enabling Brooke. All the things she stole and the lies she told me were unimaginable for me to believe. I had to finally accept it then, just like I accept it now.

2. Pain and Guilt

The implausible pain of losing a child to a drug overdose, or in any manner, is something no parent will ever get over. It is the type pain totally unexplainable to anyone who has never been where we are. For those of us who know, first hand, the pain is a topic we don't have to explain to each other. I associate this to a soldier who has been in serious battles somewhere. The soldier will not talk about what he has dealt with to just anyone, because if you weren't there, you wouldn't understand. If a person understands, then they need no explanation. If you don't understand, it could never be explained in a suitable way.

The worst thing we can do is keep all the pain bottled up inside us. It is like plugging up a volcano. Eventually, the volcano is going to erupt and the effects will be worse because of being stifled. As soon as a person is able to find a group with others who are dealing with the same issues, the sooner this person can get through the stages.

I have almost 26 years of my life invested in my daughter. That is almost 26 years of love, laughter, happiness, and excitement, which is only a memory now. I have spent sleepless nights with her while she was sick. I was there for her first broken heart. I was the one who was by her side during every major event in her life. Case and point, I was the one who had to explain her monthly cycle, and take her to buy her first sanitary napkins. Her mother was too embarrassed to talk to Brooke about these things, so Daddy did it.

I remember this talk very well. When she told me she needed some pads, I took her to the store. I thought there were a few items to choose from, but was shocked to find an entire aisle dedicated to them. I looked around some something I knew nothing about and found a small box. I thought small box for a small child. Sounds feasible, right? Wrong. Small box meant a few large ones folded small. When Brooke applied the napkin, she came out of the bathroom looking like she was straddling a large pillow. She waddled up to me and said, "Daddy, I think we got a problem." I had to call my sister, and not her mother, to rescue her from the awkward predicament I had put her in.

I had a difficult time explaining the "birds and the bees" to my sons, but it was a cake walk in comparison to having the same talk with my daughter. Topics such as these are items a father should not have to talk with his daughter about. I am not sure if her mother was too shy, or didn't want to bother talking with Brooke about certain topics. But she didn't, so everything was left to me. These talks were difficult, but I have confidence they brought us to a point where we could discuss almost anything with each other. We discussed everything except the drug usage.

I live with the guilt of enabling my daughter. I wanted to do everything I could to help her. I also have to live with guilt from thinking I didn't do enough. It has taken some time for me, and it will for you, to realize that we did all we could do for our child.

I allowed myself get into serious financial trouble over helping Brooke. I am still working on some bills I incurred while helping her, and will pay on them for yet a while. I should have never made arrangements to pay some of her court fines and let her figure her own way to pay for them. I just couldn't stand to see her worry about paying or going to jail.

From the beginning of her addiction, our relationship became a "give and take" relationship. It being the more I gave, the more she took. Much of the time she was taking without my knowledge.

One thing we, as parents, must not do, is get to the point of neglecting ourselves.

We help all we can, but we must realize that we have to keep our sanity and the ability to provide for ourselves other family members. My family suffered because I devoted too much time, energy, and money to Brooke. I felt guilty because I was sure she got into drugs because I was not there to help her make the right choices. I know now that she would have started "using," if I had been there or not. With her getting into drugs via prescription pain pills, nothing would have prevented it. Nothing I could have done would prevent Brooke's intestine disorder, and nothing would have kept her from getting the pain pills.

3. Anger and Bargaining

Anger will be prevalent in the beginning. More aptly, it will be prevalent until we overturn it. It is a human emotion that must be dealt with. Anger was the worst emotion I felt. It was also the hardest I had to deal with, yet the easiest to overcome. It will be present until we can find some type of outlet to let it go.

For the first few months after losing Brooke, I was mad at the world. The world did nothing to upset me, but I didn't care. I got mad at myself for not seeing any signs that were showing, concerning her problem. I first had to find the root cause of my anger. It was not that Brooke was gone, as I never got angry at her.

I never got angry with God for taking her. I realized I was angry with myself for allowing things, which I had no control over, to happen. Then, I was angry at myself when I realized I could do nothing to change these same events, which were not even my fault. I went a step further than just being angry. I let my anger turn into hatred.

For me, hatred was a feeling more than an emotion. It was harder to control than anger, and had to be snuffed out quickly. I hated everything and everyone. The hatred I felt was deeper than anything I have ever experienced. I struggled with feelings of anger when people tried to console me. They would tell me things like, "I am sorry for your loss," or the remark I got more than once, "I know the pain you are feeling." I understand that people were just trying to help me. I have come to appreciate that. But at first, these remarks would tend to send me over the edge.

The hatred I felt kindled a fire deep within me that was an endangerment to my very own life, and it needed to be extinguished immediately. I realized that both the anger and hatred I had within me were geared toward me. I was angry with myself, and hated myself for reasons beyond my control. I was letting it spill onto some wonderful people who were trying to help me. If I let it burn, it would have destroyed my soul and my walk with God.

Hatred came close to costing me some very dear people, who have been in my life since I was young. I had to work diligently to make amends with several family members and friends. In retrospect I see they were trying to help me through a very difficult time. But I didn't want them anywhere around me.

Unless you have lost a child, you have no idea how I am feeling. I had to pray for God to give me peace over being told someone knows what I am going through. I realize they were meant to be words of sympathy, but I took it as an offence. It is at times like these when people are truly at a loss for the right words. They try their best to convey their genuine concern.

It was difficult for me to go through this stage. But, at this time I hated everything anyway. I am not an angry person, but I was then. Sometimes, it is better to say nothing to someone dealing with a distraught mind.

Many people asked if I got mad at Brooke for leaving. After thinking about that very question several times, I can say that while being angry at the world, I never got irate with her. She was my baby and she was suffering from a disease. How does one go about getting mad at someone with a disease they can't overcome by themselves? I have also been asked if I got mad at God for taking her.

Once again, I have to say no. I prayed passionately for Him to heal my baby from her problem. Prayers were sent up, that whatever it took, please heal my daughter from her addiction. He answered my prayer, not in the way I wanted, but how He wanted.

Ephesians 1:11, says, "In whom we have also obtained an inheritance, being predestined according to the purpose of Him who worketh all things according to the council of His own will."

God did exactly what I asked Him to do. On Wednesday morning, May 23, 2018, Brooke woke up a heroin addict, and on Wednesday afternoon, of the same day, she went to sleep and into eternity, completely free and healed. How could I get mad at God for answering my prayers? God did not ask me how I wanted Him to heal her. He never gave me a chance to voice my opinion. God never asks anyone for advice or permission.

Brooke and God were the two biggest factors for me to show anger toward, but were the only two I didn't get mad at. If there is anything in her death that I am grateful for, is knowing that she felt no pain. She simply injected the deadly toxin, went to sleep, and within 2 minutes was gone.

4. Depression

Depression is a very real part of grieving. This condition and I are on a first name basis. When a life you helped create and loved unconditionally is suddenly snatched from your very arms, there will be anger and a perpetual void in your heart. There are no words to truly comfort, and no one knows the chronic pain a parent is feeling, except another parent enduring what you and I are going though. Lying in bed, I hear her voice. I see her face in the clouds. I see her playing the piano at church. I think about her all day while I am working. The list goes on and on. When I realize that all I hear or see are memories locked inside my heart, and will be all I ever have, depression again kicks me down.

It is not a bad thing to admit to being depressed. Denying one's depression is a dangerous situation to be in. Doctors will listen to what you have to say and will prescribe some type of anti-depressant. Believe me, when I tell you they actually do work. Anti-depressants work in relieving the depressive stage we are in, but they will not take the pain away. No medicine will eradicate the pain we feel through to our very soul.

Doctors will sometimes prescribe a medication to enable a person to temporarily relieve the anguish for things, such as a funeral or memorial service. Once the medication wears off, the pain will return. I had a friend who lost her mother. They were very close, and her mother's death nearly destroyed her. When I spoke with her at the funeral, she was completely dazed out of her head. I asked her father what was wrong, and he told me the doctor had given her a shot of something to "make her not care," to help her get through the most difficult day of her life.

My entire family worried over my health for fear that a heart attack would take me out. Their fear stemmed from the hospital visit I had when Brooke was doing her 90-day vacation. It could have easily happened. Early in the initial shock and denial stage, I would have been alright if that had happened.

I am not one to contemplate doing myself any danger, but at the time, death would have been alright. I actually prayed for God to remove me from this world. I prayed earnestly over this, until one day, I felt as if God spoke to my heart. I was told that my time was not yet. I have a mission to complete, and when that mission is done, I will go home.

Imagine a day, sometime in the future, when we think we are getting a handle on our depression, only to walk into a room, or anywhere for that matter, and are reminded of our child. I have walked into a store at the mall and smelled the cologne Brooke wore. Before I knew what was going on, I found myself looking around for her. I was searching intently and then realized she was not there. I have heard songs on the radio that she used to play and sing. Every time I feel like I am beginning to overcome my depression, I am reminded that I have not even come close to beating it.

During the first month of her passing, I started looking at things through eyes that didn't seem to want to function properly. Everything I did or places I visited seemed like a bad dream.

I had difficulty distinguishing reality from make believe. Things I knew were real, I now questioned. My eyes played tricks on me by showing me things that were not there. I remember a few nights after Brooke passed, I went outside to get some air, and I thought I saw people in my front yard. I got my flashlight and went back out. There was no one or nothing there.

I once saw a pack of coyotes walking toward the house late one evening. Again, I got my flashlight, only to find an old cat sitting on the wooden fence beside my house. It is difficult when a person gets to a point that they can't trust their own eyesight. The only place my eyesight was perfect was at work.

Work had become a place of solitude for me. It had become my "getaway place." It was also one of the very few places I felt safe. I can contribute all this to my depression. My very existence was meaningless, and I didn't realize that life was moving ahead without me. Nor, did I even care. I was just hanging onto what little bit of sanity I had left.

Now, that I have accepted things for what they are and realized that nothing is going to bring my daughter back, I am beginning to see things in a new perspective. It is a cold, hard fact that there are things in this world we can't change, nor understand. More on this subject will be discussed later.

Please be mindful of depression, as it can slip up on a person unnoticed. Depression can make a person see and do things that one never thought was possible. This sounds a lot like drugs, doesn't it? There have been many people that have committed suicide because their depression became so bad they felt it was their only method of escape. It was like an enemy sneaking up on me from behind. I never felt myself getting depressed. I never noticed the subtle changes in my life. By the time I realized depression was upon me, it was almost too late

Depression is still with me, but it is in check. I went to the doctor several months ago about the depressive state I was in. He prescribed some medication for me. I also told him I had started eating heavily again. About a year before Brooke passed, I started losing weight to improve my health, and after she left, I started putting it back on. This is another problem I attribute to depression.

He gave me a prescription of a medicine called Naltrexone®. He told me the mixture of the Naltrexone® and the anti-depressant I was on would act as a strong suppressant. It sounded very much like the Naloxone®, so I did some investigating on it and found it is the generic form of Naloxone®. Both Naloxone® and Naltrexone® are opioid antagonists.

Naloxone® will reverse an overdose, while Naltrexone® suppresses the desire to take opioids. I thought how ironic it is that I am taking something to battle drugs, though I have never used opioids. I spoke with the pharmacist about the medicine and told her I was taking the medicine that could have potentially saved my daughter. She told me, "Yeah, pretty much."

The only time I can recall of having any opioid in my system was when Brooke was serving her 90-day sentence. After receiving her call telling me she loved me and was going to jail for 90 days, I started hurting in my chest. I went to the hospital and found out I was in the midst of a heart attack. I was immediately admitted and the next day was scheduled for a heart catheterization.

The doctor explained the procedure that I would have, and was told I would be receiving a stent in an artery leading to my heart. I was told I would be sedated with morphine and would feel nothing.

Before the procedure began, I was then told I would feel the top of my head get extremely hot when the morphine reacted in my blood stream. I didn't know what to expect and instantly felt as though someone had placed a torch to my head. Then, I went completely out, and woke up as they were wheeling me back to my room.

I have often wondered why a person would pay money for something to be injected into their veins to simply put them to sleep. I can get the same results from over-the-counter sleep aides, and it is a lot less dangerous.

5. Upward Turn

My upward turn started when I allowed God to once again become the focal point of my life that He had been. My life had begun spiraling incessantly out of control from neglecting my Spiritual needs. Next was when I started going to Celebrate Recovery. My sister's friend invited me, and was persistent in her inviting. (Now that I look back, I am so glad she was.) She assured me it would help immensely.

How could it help me? I was neither an addict nor an

alcoholic. In my mind, I had no problem that would merit my going to such a place. I really didn't see how my talking about my daughter to a complete group of strangers would help anything, but I was very mistaken. Although talking about my hurt was difficult, it served to begin the process of my healing. My life has been changed by Celebrate Recovery. My life was spared by the caring and concern of the wonderful people there.

Before I started my road to recovery, I thought I was the only parent who had ever felt this type of pain. I know you have felt it, too. But, we must understand there are others living in the same situation as you and me. Each one is dealing with things, just like we are. With so many people dying daily from overdoses, there are parents starting their own expedition that you and I have been enduring for some while. It is my responsibility to help whomever I can in dealing with this pain. It will soon be an action you should be willing to share with others.

I remember times I attempted to talk with God about my loss. I didn't think I could talk with Him about something like this. I mean, this was my child, and He is God. Then, He reminded me that drugs snatched Brooke from my arms, but He willingly let His son hang on a cross and die for me. Wow! That put things into perspective quickly to me. God surely knows the pain of losing a child, so who better to talk with on the subject?

The road is long and hard, but when accompanied by others who share the same heartaches and hurts, it is easier to travel.

We will walk side by side, and hand in hand, sharing and caring. We will get through this easier when we are beside someone dealing with the same issue.

Just like an addict in recovery must take things "one day at a time," we must also do the same. No person wakes up one morning and is an instant addict. The same goes for parents who have lost a child. No parent will wake up one morning and be completely over their loss.

Individual circumstances differ from one to another. There is no rule stating it takes exactly the same number of months for every individual to get through the stages. What might take me a few months to get through, someone else may be ready to move on in a few weeks.

Others may struggle for years in the same stage. But, in time, we will all make it through, if we allow it. I am reminded of a question I heard many years ago. The question is: How does one eat an elephant? The answer is: One bite at a time. This is the same. Time is the element we need most throughout our stages. Time doesn't make all things better; rather it makes them more tolerable.

6. Reconstruction and Working Through

I am in the process of rebuilding my life. One day, I had three children, and the next day, I had only two. I have been told that if a person loses a limb from their body, the strength from that limb goes to the other limbs. The love we have for the child we lost will always remain strong, but the love we have for our other children will be stronger. Each of my children made up one third of my world. I now have two sons, each now making one half my world. I still love my daughter and always will. But, the love that I now feel for my sons and my granddaughter is much stronger and deeper than ever. It is like we have bonded all over.

In rebuilding my life, I have had to learn to open my heart and share the new love I have inside. The love for my family and friends is deeper, and it is easier to show them. It is an upsetting thought to know I have never dreamed of my daughter. But then again, I have not dreamed of my father since his passing. I don't have to dream of either of them because they are still alive in my heart. I see her face in the clouds; I hear her voice in the wind. Sometimes, I hear the birds calling out her name.

The love and caring I have developed for others is

noticeable to people around me. I have been told I am different person after losing my baby. I ask if that is a good or bad thing, and I have been told the change is very good. Loving and compassion have become the biggest changes in my life. It is undeniable that grief will change a person, but it is up to that person to insure the change is for the better. We do have control over that.

Job 14:1 says, "Man that is born of a woman, is of few days and full of trouble."

Every person on earth has a certain number of days to enjoy life. I have complete faith in my God, and know I will see Brooke once again. Death is the only thing standing between us, and death is the final stage of life. As much as I would love to see her again, I would not have her back living in the hell she was in. She is in a much better place and is happy and totally healed. She is the only child I have, in whom there is no need to worry about, and she is finally home.

I know I will see her again one day, but I am in no hurry to take that trip. I have too much unfinished business to take care of. God knows my departure date, and I am glad I don't. If we did know the date our final breath will be drawn, how much of our present life would be changed? We need to understand that we need to live like every breath we take will be our last.

My sons and my granddaughter are still with me, and they consume my every thought and prayer. By praying for my family, I have learned to be more open and tolerant to the needs and the concerns of others. I see each person for what they are; someone's son or daughter. I pray for them as such. Every addict is deserving of prayer for the struggle they are facing.

Don't condemn the addict, but don't condone the addiction. The road to recovery is a long, hard, and dangerous road. The demon is waiting around every corner for someone to fall. Everyone will fall at times, but the secret to success is to get up as fast as we can and continue walking. Never give up. We must never allow the dark side to know how tired we are.

As difficult as it was, I had to force myself to come to the point in which I could forgive my daughter. This was hard but something that had to be done. I had to forgive her for stealing from me, for lying to me, for causing me the worries she did, and countless other topics. Most importantly, I had to forgive her for leaving me.

Although I was never mad at her for leaving, I felt I still needed to absolve her. How could she do this to me? Why did she leave me when there was so much more I wanted to do with her and talk with her about? I didn't have to forgive her for her death as I know this was not her plan, but the end result of her taking the heroin. The drug made the decision for her.

Once I was able to forgive her, I could forgive myself, then others. After coming to this point, acceptance and hope were easier to walk through. Being able to forgive myself was more difficult than forgiving Brooke. I loved her enough to do everything I could to help her, even though she was treating me badly.

I had to learn to forgive myself of enabling her, getting mad at the world, climbing into a hole and letting life pass me by. The ability to forgive myself was a challenging obstacle I had to overcome. I had no idea how to forgive myself for something that was truly not of my doing. Once I was able to forgive myself, my life started coming back together.

We all have to come to terms with our lives and be able to forgive ourselves. This is a stipulation if we are to ever plan on forgiving others. As I have found out, and you will too, life is too short and far too precious to hold a grudge against anyone.

7. Acceptance and Hope

It has taken quite some time to come to a place in my walk that I have accepted the fact that Brooke is gone. One day, you will also come to the same place of acceptance over your child being gone. We don't have to like it. We don't have to agree with it. We simply have no alternative other than accepting it.

I spent most of my adult life delivering hospital equipment to homes of sick people. On more than one occasion, the person I delivered items to would end up passing away. I tried my best to console and comfort the family members left behind. I would tell them I lost my father in 1998, and knew the pain they were going through of losing a parent or grandparent. I never told them I knew the pain they felt from losing a child, because at that point, I didn't know the pain.

They would all, predictably, ask the same question, "How do you get over it?" My answer was always the same then, and it is exactly what I say now. You will never get over it. You have to accept it and make "friends" with the idea they are gone. If you are unable to make friends with this, be ready, because it will take you down. We all have to realize that we must be strong enough to avoid be taken completely down.

At this point in our situation, we must be as strong and vigilant as we can. We are hurting tremendously, but we are still alive. There are still other family members who are suffering and need our help. It is overwhelming to realize, but the truth is, that we lose people in our lives. Life will continue to go forward around us.

One thing to always remember is we can't become so overburdened with things that cause us to develop health problems.

It is hard enough to overcome our situation and re-focus

our energy to something else, if we are completely healthy.

I have had a difficult time deciding where to put this next bit. It would probably fit nicely under the shock and denial category, but it fits better under acceptance and hope. I mean, I know Brooke is gone and is never coming back. People have asked me why I have often referred to Brooke's passing as "left." The word "death" has certain finality to it. I see it as once dead, a person is gone forever. I simply say that she left.

Let me explain my position in this way of thinking. If we are true born again Christians, we know we will see our loved ones again. The way I see things is, she has really just traveled ahead, or left, for another place in another realm of life. She is there waiting on me to join her. I feel she has talked with my father, and both of them are waiting for the rest of the family. We will all go, one by one, until we are all together once again. She has just moved to another residence, which makes me feel that she has just left. Now, almost a year after her passing, I still have a difficult time with words like dead, passed away, deceased, and late. It is still easier for me by merely saying she left.

Through acceptance and hope, I have developed a new respect and understanding for law enforcement officers. I would not have their job for any amount of money. The only time I had any dealings with them was when they came to the house to pick Brooke up or serve some type paper on her.

I hated seeing them and was beginning to have a strong aversion to them. They had done nothing to me, but were distressing my daughter. The only time I had face to face interaction with one was when he was telling me about Brooke. I hated this man more than anyone or anything. Since then, and through much prayer and seeking God for direction, I have developed a passion to pray for these officers.

I wanted to be a police officer all my younger life. I

thought it was the coolest job anyone could ever have. I watched all police shows on television and envisioned myself in a police car going to a robbery scene or chasing a car down the highway. For many years I envisioned myself as a David Starsky (Starsky and Hutch, for those who don't remember the show) kind of guy. I wanted a red Torino with that white stripe, so bad. Man, this is the greatest thing ever, or so I thought.

I never imagined the part of the job that had to do with working a wreck in which someone died. I never thought about the horrible responsibility an officer has in telling parents their child overdosed on something and is gone. I didn't see the part where they had to leave grieving parents totally distraught. I appreciate every officer for the job they do.

When I have an opportunity to speak with an officer, I do. I walk up to one, stick out my hand, give my name, and proceed to tell them about Brooke. I tell them I have made it a personal mission to meet as many officers and let them know I pray for them daily. I tell the individual officer I am speaking with that I pray for his or her safety and pray that God allows them to safely return to their home and to the family they said goodbye to that morning.

It is astonishing to see how these officers respond to this. I have left many of them with tear-filled eyes and trembling voices. Every officer has told me they appreciate my kind words and prayers. Police officers have a very difficult job to perform. They place their lives on the line for us every day and deal with the almost criminal lack of respect toward them. I thank each officer for what they do in keeping me and my family safe. In a world such as we live in today, many times, law enforcement are made out to be criminals. I don't feel this way, and I make sure each officer I come in contact with knows exactly how I feel.

During the onset of my loss, the only hope I had was that God would soon take me out of this world. I saw my life as not worth living anymore. I was down, depressed and saw myself as being of no use to anyone. I had given up. I was ready to die myself. I didn't care. I found myself struggling to accomplish the easiest of tasks. My brain had shut down and my body didn't seem to notice. My eyes were open, but my sight was diminished. I saw nothing around me except my job and my home. I saw my job because it was the only place, other than the house, I wanted to be. I went to work, did my job, came home, ate dinner, and got ready for bed...all out of mechanical movement.

I was unaware of my surroundings and didn't notice what was going on. My mind was numb, and I saw nothing and felt less. My family was there for me, but I didn't need them (I thought), because I had no idea what I was doing. I felt like I had become the zombie type that everyone has heard about. I am amazed that I could drive to and from work safely, as many days I didn't even remember driving.

Now that I have had time to start healing, my hope has turned around. My hope is that I may be allowed to help as many people possible in the time I have left. Keep your faith in God and realize that in time, your depression will turn to hope. The only hope I had early in my grieving stage was for God to take me out of this world to escape the pain.

After surviving the grief and pain, I see more opportunity to help, because I now see more people needing it. I am not sure if I didn't see, or I was just oblivious to the fact that people from all walks of life were struggling or hurting. I see them everywhere now. I understand I am one man, who can never save the entire world, but I will do what I can to save one, then another, and then another.

Since I have started thinking with a clear mind again, I am thankful God didn't take me from this world. Although I know my days are numbered, I will use each of them to fight what took my baby from me. At the onset of this horrible event, I felt weak and useless. Now that I am healing, I realize I am not only passionate about helping others, but that I am upset to the point of being angry at the very thing that took her. I have a love for the addict, but an intense abhorrence for the drug.

We go through all the stages of grieving, and eventually will get through Step 7. Although all stages are different, they are somewhat connected. There is no set time limit we must have in each stage. This all depends on the individual and the help they receive.

When we have managed to make it through the first four stages, our healing will begin. It usually takes getting through the depression and into the upward turn. In my case getting involved with a support group and talking to parents, who are going through what you and I are dealing with, started my upward turn. Through the grieving of a loved one, doors will open, and you will begin to find the real you. For some unknown reason, the parent often finds some type of special calling in their lives, usually placed by God. I know the calling I found is to help as many as I can by giving encouragement in their travels on recovery and talking with parents on their loss. It is just a shame that I had to lose my baby to find out what my calling is.

My prayer is that this book gives you strength and courage to stay the course. The road we walk on is difficult, but understanding what is happening around you and keeping your faith in God will take you to the end of your struggle.

CHAPTER 7

The healing process is completely different from the grieving process. We go through grieving at the onset of the passing of our loved one. We hurt, we cry, we become unaware of our surroundings, we crawl into a hole inside our own body to hide. Grieving is horrible to say the least, but it is something that we will get through, if we don't give up on ourselves.

Many years ago, I had a friend that lost his son to a car wreck. It was a horrific ordeal to watch him give up on his life. All of his friends tried to help him any way we could. Without his knowledge, we would plan cookouts at his house and simply show up on the given date.

Someone in our group would call to check on him and ask if he had plans for a certain weekend. He never had plans for any weekend. He would have never invited us to anything such as this. We did our best to involve him in any group activities because he was a good friend, and we hated seeing the deterioration that had engulfed his life. Even though he would be there physically, he was mentally a million miles away.

I watched my friend go through the stages of grief, and

lose his way during the depression stage. He was never able to overcome his depression, because he couldn't let go of the grief. Within three years of losing his son, my friend became an alcoholic. He lost his job, lost his family, lost all of his friends, except me, totally lost his way, and eventually took his life. He tried dealing with the problem on his own.

This was a tragic way for my friend to finalize his life. It was also unnecessary, for he had friends and family trying to help him, yet he chose to shut them out. If you ever get to a place in your journey to think you don't need help, you are in danger of losing yourself.

If we are unable to get through most of the grieving, we will never get through to the healing. No parent who has ever lost a child will ever get completely through the grieving, nor will they be healed completely. A major step in healing understands that part of our lives is gone forever. We need to find some type way to help fill that horrible void with something beneficial to us. As hard as it was for me to talk about losing my child, I learned that talking about this very thing would be more beneficial than I ever imagined.

When we get through all the stages, it is time for us to help others. Helping others will help the healing within us. Nothing we can do or say will justify losing our child. Through the horror, we have survived in spite of feeling we never would. In going through this, we have attained vast amounts of experience and knowledge to help others wandering aimlessly along the pathway. We did not survive to keep silent about what we have been through. The more we continue to help others, the more healing we will do.

It is a fact that people come into our lives, and people leave our lives. How well we perceive their leaving, determines the outcome for our future. If one gives up and gives in to the loss, it will be difficult to gain the healing victory we all need. We must all fight to keep our sanity. I fought long and hard for mine, but it was worth it. God never expects us to simply throw in the towel. He knows, better than we do how much pain and pressure we can take. When we feel like He has left is when it becomes apparent that He is closer to us than ever.

> *Proverbs 16:20 states, "He that handleth a matter wisely shall find good: and whoso trusteth in the Lord, happy is he."*

Get involved in something productive. It doesn't matter what it is, just getting involved will help take some of the loneliness away. Understand that no matter what we do, or where we go, nothing will take it all away. Getting involved keeps the mind busy, and it will help us from growing sedentary. It motivates us to stay busy, and when we are busy, we forget some of the pain we are dealing with.

I was a Scoutmaster for many years. During the onset of my grieving, I struggled to focus my energy toward our troop, but to no avail. Although I tried to work with the Scouts, the wound was fresh and my emotions were hard to handle. I gave up my position because I felt I was not doing a good job in directing young minds in Scouting. I had not gone through grieving process completely and felt I was more of a liability to my troop.

How I deeply remember one girl getting extremely upset because there were no girls allowed in Boy Scouting. She was persistent in her desire of becoming a Scout. She didn't understand why she couldn't "go camping and do Scouting stuff." I told her it was against policy, and she didn't like that answer. She wanted to be a Scout more than anything.

This young lady was friends with all the boys in the troop, and they said it would be alright if she wanted to tag along. I had to put my foot down and tell them I could not allow it. The girl finally gave up and decided to stay home from all meetings. I knew I had upset her, but what could I do? I talked with her later that night and explained it would not look right for her to go on campouts with a bunch of guys. She listened, but still didn't like what I had to say. The girl was my daughter.

I often wonder if it would have made a difference in roads she chose to follow. I have thought about scouting a lot since quitting. I have talked with people at the Scouting Office and let them know I want to return one day as some type of counselor or commissioner. I am not sure I am, or will ever be, ready to resume my place as the head of a group of young men. I am more interested in visiting various troops and talking about the dangers of drugs.

Drugs are prevalent everywhere, and Scouting is no different. These young minds need to know what is waiting on them if they start down this path of destruction. It is our duty to love and protect all of our children. Drugs are prevalent everywhere, and in all walks of life. It is unfathomable to think that elementary school age children have been introduced to drugs, but I know of several instances where they have.

While I was Scoutmaster, I also worked with Cub Scouts. These young Cubs ranged from age 5 to 11. One of the requirements for them to advance was to participate in a meeting discussing the dangers of drugs. I remember the first such meeting I arranged. I was also acting as Cubmaster, and had scheduled a police officer with his drug sniffing dog to visit with us. I introduced him to the boys and told them how his dog was going to show how he finds drugs.

As soon as I mentioned this, several parents got up and immediately left the meeting area. The officer proceeded to show the Scouts exactly how his dog tracked down hidden drugs. The dog was incredible, as he found a very small amount of Marijuana, hidden by the officer in the back corner of a file cabinet. It didn't take the dog long to find it. Officer Smith explained how police dogs are trained and how officers are trained to work with dogs. When a dog is sniffing for drugs, it is actually sniffing for its favorite toy.

On a personal note, if you ever see a "cop" show, in which the dog is holding a suspect by the arm and swinging him around, and you think to yourself there is no way a little dog could do that to a big man, believe it. Officer Smith silently asked me if I would be willing to help in the next part of his demonstration, and without hesitating, I said yes. Officer Smith asked to boys if they would like to see his dog attack me. WHAT? What did I just volunteer to do?

Officer Smith explained what he wanted me to do. The part I remember most was him telling me not to move, whatever, don't move. This was not going to be a problem, since I was already frozen stiff with fear. I donned the safety gear and prepared myself to have a dog lunge at me. As soon as Officer Smith gave the command, his dog hurled itself at me and firmly attached itself to my left arm.

I guess it must have been a funny site, to everyone except me, to see a 275-pound man being swung around like a rag doll by a 90 pound Belgian Malinois. Officer Smith proceeded to talk with the boys as the dog dangled from my arm. Just as quickly as he had given the command to attack, he gave a command and the dog released me.

The meeting was a big success and people thanked Officer Smith for the show. I told him about the parents leaving as soon as he brought his dog in. We laughed and discussed having officers at both doors waiting for exiting parents. One thing I would like to inject here is what Officer Smith told me after the meeting, while he and I were the only two left. He told me I was lucky that his dog got traction when he launched.

He proceeded to tell me many times a dog can't get good traction on tile floors. If the dog had not gotten the traction needed to make a good attack jump, he would have slipped and bit me anywhere he could have gotten hold. This was a great relief for me knowing I was at the mercy of a dog not slipping. I don't think I would have been so eager to be used, had I known this.

I am sure Officer Smith was thinking about the floor the entire time, but was simply keeping that little morsel of information secret until after the meeting. As I was locking the church up, I discovered I was still trembling with fear. It is not often I am asked to allow a police dog to dangle from my arm. I could tell mine was not the first arm this dog had latched onto.

During my tenure as Scoutmaster, the size of the troop would grow then dwindle. Our troop ranged from between 8 and 25 boys, between 11 and 18 years of age. We had a lot of young men come and go. One thing in common for the leaders is we are always running into someone who spent time in the troop.

It is wonderful to reminisce about camping trips past. We talk sometimes for half an hour, we laugh, we hug and say goodbye. I have relived trips with these great guys on many occasions. Sometimes, I enjoy the memories more than the actual trip.

For close to 15 years, I was responsible for taking care of between 10 and 40 young minds with ages ranging from 5 to 18 years. I would like to think that in that time, we, the leaders, made a difference in at least one life.

I feel that in order for us to understand what our child went through, we must know what they dealt with on a daily basis. We need to explore exactly what took them from us. Military strategists have formulated the theory that in order to conquer one's enemy, one must study and understand that enemy. I decided to explore the ways opioids work in the body. My research findings are almost unbelievable. I was totally amazed at what I found. Let me share with you, what I have found.

Americans make up only five percent of the world's population, but use 80 percent of all opioids. In 2016, there were over 64,000 deaths in the United States from drug related overdoses, with the majority coming from opioids. There were over 70,000 deaths in 2017. In these two years alone, that is over 134,000 deaths. If we factor in the ones left behind to grieve, it could be well over a quarter of a million people impacted by drug overdoses.

I am not a doctor and hold no type of degree. I will explain what I have discovered in a way that is easily understood. If you want to know more about what our children dealt with, the internet is full of information more in depth than explained here. If you don't have computer access, you can find information at any recovery meeting, or even the family doctor can give you information.

CHAPTER 8

The opioid addict's brain becomes very complex. It becomes totally "re-wired" toward the addiction. It becomes a physical dependency to the drug. Opioids affect the pleasure sensing part of the brain, called the Frontal Cortex. This is where all feelings of reward and euphoria come from. It is also the part of the brain that deals with motor function and compulsion.

The brain produces chemicals called endorphins. This peptide chemical is produced when pain or high stress are introduced to the body. It is like a naturally produced morphine that helps control pain and triggers the "feel good" circuits of the brain. When heroin, or any other opioid, is introduced, it sends an incredible surge into the same circuits. These circuits become overloaded. The brain regulates the endorphins, and when the surge is introduced, it throws the system off.

Dopamine is a chemical in the brain that sends messages from one brain cell to another. This chemical tells the brain that taking the drugs is a good thing, and it should repeat it. Life without taking the drug becomes difficult and stress and irritability become unmanageable. More drugs are then needed to fend these off. The person takes more drugs and it is not as euphoric as the first "high," so more drugs are taken. It becomes a vicious cycle. Before long, the circuits in the brain are re-wired in that the pleasure and reward circuits are reversed. They will get less "high" each time it is used, but they will want it more. They come to reasoning that, since they are not as "high," they need to increase the amount of drug.

The brain soon gets adapted to the drug and the amount is increased again. Before long, drugs are needed just for the addict to feel normal. The first "high" an addict gets from opioids is the best one they will ever have. They will actually use and increase dosage to try to get another "high" as good as the first one, which will never happen. This is why addicts increase their dosages. It becomes a "Catch 22" in that more drugs are needed to feel good, and the body becomes resistant to the amount that is taken, so the dosage has to be increased again.

When an addict decides to stop taking their drug of choice, they may not even know how addicted to it they are. They stop taking it, and soon withdrawal symptoms start. The symptoms can go from mild to extremely difficult. Sleeplessness, vomiting, pains, hot and cold flashes, and congestion are some symptoms. When compiled on top of anxiety and depression, many feel as though they are going to die.

I have been around addicts for a while now, and have never heard of any person dying from not taking drugs. They may feel like it, but they will get through it. I have learned it is not as easy as just laying drugs down and walking away. Just like Brooke, the pain was more than she could handle. The demon would not turn her loose. She had to have that one last "high," and took heroin that was laced with fentanyl, and in reality, it actually was her last "high."

Although I have never looked at the official death report, my sister told me it stated that from the time of injection to time of death was less than 2 minutes. She had locked herself in the bathroom and locked both doors of the house where she and her fiancé lived. Even if someone had been with her, there would have not been enough time for the paramedics to arrive and save her.

For the addict who is blessed enough to make it through the initial withdrawal, there are months of feeling like they need to get "high" just to function. All the while, the brain is beginning to "re-wire' itself to its original functioning capabilities. No outside endorphins are being introduced and life is slowly returning to a somewhat regular state. No dopamine is telling the brain that drugs are good. It takes quite a while for the brain to return to normal. Sometimes, it can take from 18 to 24 months for regular brain activities to return.

There are drugs available to help with the withdrawals. They are prescribed by a physician. These drugs help, but it is extremely important for the addict to find some type recovery program. In the program, there are other addicts to talk with and help. They have walked the road and lived. Addiction simply means that we become dependent to anything that alters the brain to give us pleasure.

I know drug addicts, alcoholics, and tobacco users. But, I also know exercise addicts, jogging addicts, sports addicts. My oldest son is addicted to video games. Wow, I bet that hits home with a lot of us! All my life, I have been told, "Too much of anything can be bad." As a child, I had no concept of the meaning behind this. Now as an adult, I understand this is all too true.

CHAPTER 9

The 12 Steps of Recovery, which are the same ones that alcoholics use, are just as useful to anyone affected by drugs in any way. They are also as difficult for us to work. The 12-Step Program was developed by the members of an Alcoholics Anonymous program in Akron, Ohio, in the 1930's. The steps were developed by Bill Wilson and Dr. Bob Smith.

The program has evolved into a program for more than alcoholics. It is now used for NA, or Narcotics Anonymous, gambling, depression, eating disorders, and sexual addiction programs.

Although the loss of our child may be the only thing we are suffering from, the 12-Step Program is also beneficial to us. We will discuss the program developed for Narcotics Anonymous. This program shares the 12 steps, but also gives Biblical comparisons.

Step 1

We admitted we were powerless over our addictions and compulsive behaviors, that our lives had become unmanageable.

Biblical comparison: "For I know that good itself, does not dwell in me, that is, in my sinful nature. For I have the desire to do what is good, but I cannot carry it out." (Romans 7:18)

I finally came to the conclusion that I was, indeed, powerless over the situation I was utterly thrust into. Through no deed of my own, I was cast into a pit in which I could see no way out of. My life had truly become unmanageable. I could focus on nothing of importance. My life, just like Brooke's, had begun spiraling out of control, which I didn't notice at first. I tried to do what was right, but I found myself doing the wrong things to get through all this. My right became wrong, and my wrong seemed right.

Step 2

We came to believe that a Power greater than ourselves could restore us to sanity.

Biblical comparison: "For it is God who works in you to will and to act in order to fulfill His purpose." (Philippians 2:13)

This step was particularly difficult for me as I wanted to do harm to those who had harmed my daughter. Being the father, I wanted to find them and take care of business myself. The fleshly part of me wanted to track down every drug dealer. My early actions would have resulted in my being incarcerated. I would have been no use to myself or anyone around me. I realized I would have been no better than the dealer.

Sanity was non-existent during my early stages for grief. Men are pretty much the type to act first and ask questions later. When we are stressed, it is not good to feel this way. Throughout this entire tribulation I discovered it better to be observant and study the situation rationally.

My mental instability was causing me to stray from God, and I had to gain control of it and focus on things that mattered. I know that if it had not been for my God, I would surely have lost my mind. To take it a step further, I would have lost my life. Once I let Him, God took control of my mind and ways of thinking.

Deuteronomy 32:35 states, "To me belongeth vengeance, and recompence; their foot shall slide in due time: for the day of their calamity is at hand, and the things that shall come upon them make haste."

God knows when His child is harmed and will take care of the situation in His time.

Step 3

We made a decision to turn our lives and our wills over to the care of God. When I realized I was taking the mess my life had become and making it worse, I decided to give it to God. He is the only way any part of my life could be salvaged.

Biblical Comparison: 'Therefore, I urge you, brothers and sisters in view of God's mercy, to offer your bodies as living sacrifices, holy and pleasing to God—this is your true and proper worship." (Romans 12:1)

I couldn't take any more stress, so I gave my heart to God. Once God restored my heart, the rest of my life followed. The thing God wants more than anything from us is obedience. If we become obedient to His will and His way, we grow closer to Him. Prayer, fasting, and meditation are ways to search for God's will in our lives.

I give myself completely to you my God. To do with as you please. Use me as a mighty instrument of warfare in battle. I will do as You ask of me, and stand for you at any and all cost. You gave me life, and allowed Your son's blood be shed for me. I will give you my all.

Step 4

We made a searching and fearless moral inventory of ourselves.

Biblical comparison: "Let us examine our ways and test them, and let us return to the Lord." (Lamentations 3:40)

I asked God to search my heart and show me anything I was doing wrong. I changed what He showed me, and focused my full attention in serving Him. The ways I wanted to act were not of God. They were of my own choosing and would have caused my destruction. The fleshly part of me wanted vindication immediately. I realized this temperament was wrong, and I had to humble myself and trust in my Higher Power. I grew dependent on God for His leading.

Step 5

We admitted to God, to ourselves, and to another human being the exact nature of our wrongs.

Biblical comparison: "Therefore, confess your sins to each other and pray for each other so that you may be healed." (James 5:16)

I found this to be particularly difficult. I could confess what my wrongs were to God, but it was virtually impossible to talk about them to another human. I have told some of my deepest problems and wrongs to friends I would have trusted my life with, only to find they spread our confidential conversation to others and it spread like wildfire. It is embarrassing to share my past with others, only to have someone else ask me about what I did.

Even Teresa could not be trusted by me. I shared private fragments of my life with her, and I was shocked when I next saw her brothers and they asked me things about it. I looked for quite some time to find someone I could trust with my innermost secrets. Be careful who you tell things to. I found someone I could put my trust in and their trust in me. We talk and pray for each other often.

Step 6

We were entirely ready to have God remove all these defects of character.

> Biblical comparison: "Humble yourselves before the Lord and He will lift you up." (James 4:10)

God does not like proud or haughty people. He can't do anything with a person that is so full of himself there is no room for God to dwell. I realized I had become my own worst enemy and was full of anger. I humbly asked God to help me overcome my anger and worked hard for restoration of my peace of mind.

Step 7

We humbly asked Him to remove all of our shortcomings.

> Biblical comparison: "If we confess our sins, He is faithful and just and will forgive us our sins and purify us from all unrighteousness." (1 John 1:9)

Search me, precious God, and show me anything that is standing between You and me. If there is something, give me the strength to overcome it and cast it to the ground.

For You, my God, are the reason I am here, and the reason I want to shout to the Heavens the Glory of Your righteousness.

My sins are many, and I cast them at your feet, and plead Your precious blood to cover them. Please remove my shortcomings and create in me a new heart. Please forgive me of any transgressions against you or another.

Use me as You see fit. I humbly give myself to you and to your service.

Step 8

We made a list of all the persons we had harmed, and we became willing to make amends to them all.

Biblical comparison: "Do unto others as you would have them do to you." (Luke 6:31)

I treat people the way I want to be treated. I don't like to be used, lied to, or cheated. I don't do this to others, and if I have offended anyone, I apologize and am willing to do whatever it takes to make this offence right.

I made a mental list of the people I had harmed over my life. I have actually contacted several and asked for forgiveness. Many of the ones I feel I have harmed or mistreated have passed on or moved. I have no way of finding them, so I pray that God will touch them.

Step 9

We made direct amends to such people whenever

possible, except when to do so would injure them or others.

Biblical comparison: "Therefore, if you are offering your gift at the alter and there remember that your brother or sister has something against you, leave your gift there in front of the altar. First go and be reconciled to them; then come and offer your gift." (Matthew 5:23-24)

Nothing is more important than the relationship I have with You. If I hold bad feelings within my heart, I have less room for you. Apologies are a difficult thing to give, sometimes. Having to admit the wrongs I have done, is a chore I prefer not to do. But, if doing so helps me find peace in my heart and mercy from You, I am willing.

We need to come to a point of realization that we are to treat our brothers and sisters the way we want to be treated. I like to be treated with dignity and respect, so I therefore show the same. I will not willingly cheat or wrong another human, and if I find I have innocently done so, I will make all amends to right my wrong.

Oh my Lord, let nothing stand between me and You. If I have offended my brother, show me so I can ask forgiveness of him.

Step 10

We continued to take personal inventory and, when we were wrong, promptly admitted it.

Biblical comparison: "So, if you think you are standing firm, be careful that you don't fall." (1 Corinthians 10:12)

I have been wrong many times in my life. No one is perfect and we will make mistakes and find we are in the wrong at times. It is easier to admit it as soon as they are discovered. If we wait, we will not find the time to correct it, and we will often soon forget it. Eventually, we will not remember our deed and will come to a place where we will repeat our wrong.

May God quicken my mind and let me never repeat the wrongs I have done in my past. Show me my God what is in me that needs to be brought to light so I may ask your forgiveness from.

In my past, I have pushed God for things I thought I wanted or needed. I know now that in some instances I pushed God so much that I pushed Him completely out of the way. Every time I did this, things went extremely bad. When God is not in something, it is doomed to fail. I am not perfect by any means and have no problem admitting my faults. I have failed God many times in the past.

One of my biggest failures was marrying for the second time. I met a lady, and we decided to marry. The deep love for her was not in me, but I married anyway. I didn't like the feeling of going through life alone. Brooke and this lady became very close before she and I started dating.

When things got serious between us, Brooke grew distant from me and despised her. I attributed this to simple jealousy over her father. She begged me not to marry the lady because she wasn't right for me. I never prayed, I never sought God's will for guidance concerning the impending marriage. I married without waiting on an answer from God, and soon found myself out of church, away from my children, and distanced from my family. I felt my life beginning to go down a path of corruption.

God never left my side, but gave me space and wisdom to discover my fault. I soon realized that my relationship with God, my children, and my entire family was in jeopardy, so I did something about it. I prayed for God to help me out of the mess I had made in my life, and I worked on correcting my wrong. I was divorced from this lady two years after we were married, and I worked on getting my children and family back.

It was during this marriage that Brooke moved back with her mother and started getting into pills from the hospital. I wonder if she would have ever gotten into them, if I had not taken it upon myself to change my life. This is another question I will live with. I gave my heart back to God, and I got back into church where I belonged. Pretty soon, my life started coming back together. I apologized to my children for putting them through the things that happened during that short marriage mistake.

Step 11

We sought through prayer and meditation to improve our conscious contact with God praying only for knowledge of His will for us and power for us to carry that out.

Biblical comparison: "Let the message of Christ dwell among you richly." (Colossians 3:16)

The message of Christ is to be shared with the world. We are to use it to make us better people. The more of God's word we carry in our hearts, the stronger we will be. The stronger we are, the more we can resist temptation. We must learn to listen to God and to heed His Word. God will not communicate with those who are not ready to receive His Word. The prince of darkness knows the word of God very well. When he comes against us using God's word, we must be stronger in the Word to use it against him. This only comes from studying and prayer.

Revelation 3:20 states, "Behold I stand at the door, and knock: If any man hear my voice and open the door, I will come into him and sup with him, and he with me."

God does not force Himself on anyone. We have the choice to hear His word and carry it to the rest of the world.

Step 12

Having had a spiritual experience, as the result of these steps, we try to carry this message to others and to practice these principles in all our affairs.

Biblical comparison: "Brothers and sisters, if someone is caught in a sin, you who live by the spirit should restore that person gently. But watch yourself, or you also may be tempted." (Galatians 6:1)

Although never an addict, I have now devoted my life to helping them. I talk of the dangers of drugs. I will never condemn an addict for the choices they have made, but neither will I accept their actions.

Regardless of what happened to cause an addict to be in the position he or she is in, they need help.

I do not know the horror of being an addict, but an addict doesn't know the horror you and I have been through. If they did, it might possibly be enough to sway them.

CHAPTER 10

Be careful of what you do or say, and be mindful of the environment you are in. Even the strongest of us can be pulled into situations that modify life. I once went to church with an older gentleman who was a devout Christian. He was also a recovering alcoholic.

Our church was participating in a fundraiser to add onto our building. The man turned in a lot of money he collected from selling aluminum cans. He would get them anywhere he could. He even started going to beer joints and taverns to collect the cans.

So far, he was doing alright, until he started going inside to collect cans from the trash baskets. It wasn't long until he was helping empty them. He lost his way, and became something he had worked most of his life to free himself from.

He died an alcoholic, simply from getting too close and letting temptation devour him. The story of the woman who went to the well 99 times and on the 100th trip, she fell in, stands true in this situation.

1 Corinthians 10:12 says, "Wherefore let him that thinketh he standeth take heed lest he fall."

None of us are perfect, and eventually, each of us will fall. If you do fall, get up quickly, dust yourself off, and continue on your trail. If you don't get up quickly, corruption will swallow you.

Isaiah 40:31 says, "They that wait upon the Lord shall renew their strength. They shall rise up with wings as eagles. They shall run and not be weary. They shall walk and not faint."

In everything I have been through, I have completely learned to wait upon God. It is God who directs my path and leads the way. I have given my life to Him to do as He pleases. One thing I remember richly is that from the shock and denial stage through the depression stage, I looked at the world, yet saw nothing. I mean it was like my eyes quit working correctly. I seemed to see things that were not there and didn't see things that were right in front of me.

Through much prayer and waiting on God, I seem to be seeing the world through a new set of eyes. I see things I have never noticed before. Everything seems to look sharper and the colors are much more vivid. This world is much more beautiful when we observe it through eyes He has opened. One thing I am seeing is that this world is full of people hurting and struggling. With the help of God, I have taken on the role of a caregiver. I will pray, talk with, encourage, and uplift any addict or alcoholic I find.

Waiting on God is better than praying for patience. God will sometimes send us through trials to teach us patience. Waiting on God requires listening for Him to speak to us. We must listen with our heart and be willing to do as He says. Praying for patience is asking God to send us through trials. I have enough trials in my life, and I have learned patience through them to never pray for more.

In all things I do, I totally wait on guidance from God. I have leaned on Him so much this year, I am afraid to make a move without Him in charge. I cannot, nor will not, say that losing my baby was a blessing. I will instead say that since her passing, I can see blessings coming my way. I see doors before me that God will open in His time. These doors will remain closed until He feels I am ready to go through. I will not grow impatient while waiting, for I know that He has my best interest in His control. Peace and contentment comes from waiting on Him. When God is in control of our lives, everything will be right.

Before all this came about with Brooke and her mother, my way of thinking was such that drugs are only found in the bigger cities, and drug addicts were the scum of the earth. I thought none of them could ever be trusted, and it was better to stay as far away from them as possible. My mind had me convinced that I had nothing to worry about with drugs. I knew in my heart the family was safe and secure from drugs and the lowly addict.

I began to see drug addiction in a different way. Anyone can become an addict. Addiction is no respecter of persons. People from all stages of life can become addicted to drugs. Many people start down the road of addiction much like Brooke and her mother; through prescription drugs. I have also found that there is no person walking on earth, who demonstrates more courage on a daily basis, than an addict in recovery. They have been to hell, fought the demon, and yet lived to tell about it.

I have talked with several addicts, some recovering and some active. The big difference I have noticed is that active addicts don't care if they have another day on earth or not. They seem to have given up on themselves and their lives. They get to a point where the only thing of importance is where and when they can get high again. The recovering addict is totally different. Although the recovering addict is, and always will be, addicted to drugs, they know where they are now is much better than where they were. They know when and where to get strength they need to overcome the cravings.

Not only do I feel they are the strongest people, I also feel they have an unpretentious humbleness about them. They all realize where they would be if someone had not given them a hand up. People in true recovery show a genuine concern for others in their situation. If an addict is lucky enough to find a God-based recovery program, they will soon want to lead others out of the bondage they have been in. Most of all, the recovering addict shows a sincere love for life and for God. For they know it is God that rescued them from their bondage.

Recovering addicts also know the dangers awaiting them if they relapse. I have to say it is incredibly profound to hear recovering addicts speak of the horrors they have faced. It is enough to scare the strongest of people. The only thing I have found that worries the active addict is not knowing when or where they will get their next fix.

Every addict in true recovery has my utmost admiration and deepest respect. With active addicts, it is either "high or die." In Brooke's case, as well as many others, it was "get high, and die." She hit rock bottom and wanted to get clean, but the hold the demon had on her was just too strong for her to contend with. While she only wanted to feel the "high," she had no actual intention of doing herself any bodily harm. But the drug had other plans.

It has been over a year since Brooke left, and I am no closer to getting over the pain than I was when it first happened. The pain (though somewhat less intrusive) will always be there for us all, but can be disguised in different forms. The major disguise pain has taken is that of a genuine concern for others. I have realized it is easier to deal with my own pain while helping others deal with theirs. It has been a while since I have had a smile on my face, but the pain I feel diminishes when I see a smile on the face of someone I have been trying to help. Pain also eases for me when I focus on praying for others.

This journey I have taken has dealt with many circumstances over the past year. My life has been forever changed, my walk has been altered. The path I walk now is directed by God and Him alone. I am no longer the man I was. I hope I am better in some way. I know that no matter what I do or where I go in life, nothing was worth giving my daughter up for. Just like an addict, I am on the road to recovery. My travels will continue for my duration. I am devoted to helping fight this epidemic any way I can.

One thing I can say is I still love and pray for the addict, but I still hate the drugs that made them. Just like addicts or alcoholics, we are subject to relapse. We must focus on the future, and not dwell on the past. We will continually think about our child, but there is a difference in thinking and dwelling. Images or thoughts run through everyone's mind. Some are good and some not so good.

We are all human and have active thinking. It is when we act upon some of the thoughts, they become bad. When things go bad, relapse is coming. If we live in the past, we are allowing our past to repeat itself. We all must learn from our past and focus on our future.

This journey we are on is much like that of recovery for the addict. It is not a sprint, but a marathon. This is definitely a passage of endurance. Recovery and dealing with the loss of a child take time to deal with. Both will take the rest of our lives.

Just when I thought I was beginning to reclaim the grip on my life, I heard that a very dear friend of my overdosed and passed away. The news of his passing sent me all the way back to the feelings of helplessness in the beginning. My horrible wound was re-opened and the pain, once again, became alive in my soul. My mind and body go numb at the thought of another life lost to this epidemic.

When will it stop? How many deaths are enough? Who is going to stand up and fight to help get this madness under control? My friend helped many recovering, while working hard to maintain his stability. I am not sure what provoked him to relapse and fall back into the pit he had spent almost a year climbing out of.

It just serves to show that even the strongest can stumble. When a person stumbles, the person is opening themselves up to temptation. Everyone stumbles, but it is imperative that we get up as soon as we can. If one stumbles and gives up, one gives in. If one gives in, it is game over. May God bless my friend's family. He leaves behind a wonderful wife, and their beautiful children. Just like my baby girl's situation at first, his journey has ended. He is safe, and is no longer bound by the demon that stood in the way of his being free. He is free now. Now, his wife and children start their journey.

During this year, I have learned so much, yet I have so many unanswered questions. I am sure you will be the same when you reach the one year mark of your child's passing. Several questions will go unanswered, and I will continue to live my life as best I can. A few things I have learned are that drugs are no respecter of persons. It doesn't discriminate, because they hate everyone.

Once bound by drugs, it is difficult to get clean and difficult to stay clean. Drugs are easier for our children to get than they have ever been in the past. I remember while in high school, there was not much talk about drugs, because drugs were not popular. I went completely through all four years and never heard of anything even remotely connected to drugs, although I am sure they were there.

It was not until I attended college in the early 1980's that I started hearing about drugs and overdoses. They were nowhere near as common as they are now. Although I have never taken drugs (not even pain pills that were prescribed) or even tried marijuana, I was around it. In the younger years of my life, I remember going a concert and smelling the distinct stench of "pot." I looked around to find the source and found a boy standing directly behind me, smoking it. This young man looked to be in his mid to late teens, and he was stoned out of his head. The degree of his condition caused me to feel there was more than marijuana in his system.

I didn't care, as I was young, on my own, and ready to rock to some great music. The impact of drugs and overdoses had not yet reached into my heart and ripped the very feeling of life from me. That was 40 years ago, and I find myself thinking of him from time to time. More now, since my life has ceased being the way it was. I wonder if he is still around or has he become another statistic. Did he straighten up, or did the "Reaper" claim another victim?

I know I am better than no one else, and am only here by the grace of my God. I share what I can with whomever I can, and have touched a few people through the words God places in my heart. One such person is a friend of mine. He is a struggling alcoholic, wanting help. I spoke harsh but caring words to him and told him if he didn't get help soon, death would be coming to visit. He didn't want to hear that and I know I didn't want to say it, but it was placed on my heart. I would have disrupted the spirit that gave me the words, had I not obeyed. He promised to come to Celebrate Recovery with me, and I hope he keeps his promise. His brother is an alcoholic, suffering from cirrhosis of the liver. He is not long for this world, and I told my friend he wasn't long for it either.

The impact I made in talking with my friend will be evident in the coming weeks. We can only give suggestions to the suffering. Until they are ready to receive help, they will never accept it. Whatever happens, they must understand there are supporters waiting and willing to help, no matter the time of day. But, there is a certain amount of will power and perseverance they will definitely need during this challenging time.

Overcoming any type addiction is a struggle that lasts a

lifetime. As time goes on, the severity of the struggle lessens, but will always be there to a certain extent. A note to add here is my friend came to Celebrate Recovery once, and has not been back. I see him daily and he promises he will return, but he hasn't yet. I will not keep asking him, but let him know the invitation is open.

Matthew 11:28 states, "Come unto me, all ye that labour and are heavy laden, and I will give you rest."

As we have all discovered through our ordeal, there is more than being physically weary. During times in each of our lives, we will become physically, mentally, as well as, spiritually exhausted. Nothing can cause one to become heavier laden than dealing with the loss of a child. We become useless when we are too tired to do anything. I well remember feeling completely drained of energy when Brooke passed.

Our mental capabilities diminish when our brain is worn out and begins to shut down. When our own spirituality becomes weak, we open ourselves to temptation. Temptation is never a good thing. The next verse goes hand in hand with the above mentioned. The power of God, or our Higher Power, will give us the rest we desperately seek.

Philippians 4:13 says, "I can do all things through Christ which strengtheneth me."

Both of these verses can be combined to let us know that becoming weak is not a good thing. I think back about the amount of physical strength I lost. It is difficult to stay strong when one sits in front of the television and stares at a blank screen.

Just like a bodybuilder who works out to build muscles, I had to work out to rebuild each of my strength deficits.

Our muscles have a tendency to quit working if we stop using them. Without changing my routine much, and without joining a gym, I developed methods of working my strength level. Things I do would be to park away from a store door and walk. When I mow, I do not use the self-propel feature and use more of my strength to push the mower. I would exercise to increase the blood circulation to my brain and muscles.

Although I was really not excited to start the process, physical rebuilding seemed to be the easiest. My sleep patterns were thrown off, so I adjusted my bed time and wake time. I did what I could to improve myself. Subtleties in one's routine may not seem big, but the benefit is incredible.

Mental strengthening can be as simple as working crossword puzzles. I do some of those, and I work the word search puzzles. Instead of working math problems on a calculator, I do them the old fashioned way of using a pencil and paper.

One thing I find interesting is taking bottles of household items in the kitchen or bathroom and attempting to pronounce some of the extremely large words on the back. I have no idea if I actually pronounce them right, but it causes my brain activity to increase.

Do anything you can to use your brain more and focus on things that are coming in the future. Wedding, birthdays, anniversaries, graduations; things like these. Do not dwell on the past. Simply do anything you can to increase the activities of the brain.

CHAPTER 11

Throughout all of this, emotions were more problematic to control. My heart was destroyed, so I had to attempt piecing it back together. I didn't care if I said something to hurt someone. I didn't bother to worry about those around me. I was hurting and it was fine if they were hurting, too. Luckily, I was introduced to my group family through Celebrate Recovery. They literally saved my life. It took a long time, (in fact, I am still working on this) but I endeavored to re-train my brain.

When I felt a depressive feeling coming over me, I would talk with someone. I would fill my mind with thoughts of my boys or my granddaughter. I would strive to think of the joy and happiness they bring me. I focused on the positive and not the negative. Instead of thinking about my daughter, now gone a year, I would think of my granddaughter. My mind would soon be overflowing with joyous memories, and the depression would take a back seat. If you don't believe this, try it next time you feel depression creeping in, overcoming you're thinking. It works.

My spiritual strengthening was crossed with emotional. As earlier stated, I attended the same church as Brooke and her mom. I had to overcome the feelings of them not being in church. I worked on this so much and so hard that I now am excited to go, because I can feel the presence of my daughter around me.

At first, the feeling was haunting, and somewhat terrifying. But now, I embrace it as a new peace that flows over me. I can feel Brooke with me in that Holy place. Spirituality strengthening was difficult to get back onto. But the more I did, the easier it became.

Prayer is a key element in spirituality. Study God's word and meditate on it. Set aside some daily personal time for Bible study and meditation.

Every morning it is a good idea to give yourself to God for a few minutes. Talk with Him and let Him guide your path through the day. I have found that the Bible is full of encouraging words to strengthen us. It is the particular type of reading we need to do on a daily basis. I am finding the more I fill my heart with God, the less room I have for pain and negativity.

Meditate on the positive in your life, and not the negative.

The past is exactly what it is. It is things we have done or places we have gone before. The past can serve to hinder our growth if we let it. I have told many people, "Leave the past in the past. The only person your past can hurt is you." It can cause people to lose focus on the present or even the future. We can't change the past, but we can use it to prevent us from making the same mistakes again. Learn from it, and let it go.

Memories, both good and bad, are all we have of the past. They live in special rooms in our mind. We have a room full of memories from our childhood to memories of our children. When a child becomes a memory, they are placed in a sacred room in our mind, and guarded heavily. No one is allowed to disturb this room except the one in whom it resides. There will be memories of the child that we will speak of. Other memories are reserved only for the parent. I have memories of Brooke that I share with others, while maintaining special memories only for myself and share with no one. These memories I will take to my grave with me.

A story I would like to share about Brooke was when she was 4-years-old. We had just moved into a house and I was exhausted from putting furniture together all day. I was sitting on the couch relaxing for a moment, when Brooke's older brother, Brandon, came and told me Brooke was jumping on my and her mother's bed. I told her to stop jumping. Brandon came back a few minutes later and told me the same thing again. I yelled at her to stop and thought she did. Within a few minutes Brandon repeated his story of her on the bed. I called her into the living room where I was and told her I didn't want to hear about her jumping on my bed again.

Her attitude was showing some as she went to her bedroom. Just a few minutes passed before Brandon told me she was now jumping on HER bed. I called her out of the room and scolded her. She looked at me with all seriousness she could muster, and told me, "Daddy, I was in my room, and what I do in my room is my business." This remark came from the mouth of my 4-year-old, and totally caught me off guard. I sent her to room before I burst into laughter. I asked her mother if I should punish her or just laugh it off. I scolded her, but I didn't feel right about doing it.

Another story was when I came home from work, tired and ready to relax. Brooke was 5 and was already showing her brothers who was boss. I came in and sat down on the couch to rest a few minutes before dinner. Brandon and Cody were in the back yard playing. They were having too much fun to hear me call for them to come into the house to eat. I called a little louder and nothing happened. I yelled this time, but to no avail. They were involved with playing they didn't hear me at all. I was about to get up and go get them, until Brooke patted me on my knee and said, "Don't worry hun, I'll get them." With a very loud piercing voice, she yelled for the boys to "Get in this house right now, and I mean business." She turned around and said to me, "There you go." Within a matter of a few seconds, both boys were in the house and out of breath from running in fear of retribution from Brooke.

These two memories are highly cherished by me and are the only ones I have allowed myself to share. I have more memories, but I will keep them reserved in that sacred room in my heart for me to appreciate and take to my grave.

As much as I love talking about her, whom I have only been able to do a short period, I love to hear stories shared by others. I have learned just how much my baby loved me and depended on me from some of her closest friends. Unfortunately, I was not the one she went to for help for her addiction problem. She let no one in to that side of her life, except her mother.

By the time I knew she had a problem, it was too late for me to help. She told me she wanted help one day, and the next she was gone. I know she didn't plan on dying, but she did. I will never get to walk my baby down the aisle at her wedding. I will never hold another grandchild from her. I wanted her to teach me to play piano, and she promised she would. It never happened.

Something as simple as chocolate oatmeal cookies will never be made again for me. I asked her for over a year to make me some, and although promising to do so, it never came to pass. I can hold these things against her, but what would that do? I had to let them go and cherish the memories of what she did for me. She gave me a beautiful granddaughter before leaving this world. Baylee is so much like her mother it is amazing. Her actions, demeanor, temper, and looks are all just like Brooke. I see my baby in my grandbaby.

Addiction comes in many forms other than drugs and

alcohol. Addiction simply means that we become dependent to anything that alters the brain and gives us pleasure. I know drug addicts, alcohol addicts, and tobacco addicts. But I also know exercise addicts, jogging addicts, sports addicts.

Throughout my life, I have heard the term "adrenaline junkie," but never understood its true meaning, until now. It is someone addicted to adrenaline. Excitement that causes the heart to race will cause adrenaline to be released in the body. This is an addiction.

It is time I admit to being an outdoor addict. I love to hunt, fish, camp, and anything that will get me into the woods. I have several thousand dollars tied up in the equipment of my addiction. The accumulation of my gear has taken me many years to acquire. I didn't have to steal to buy a new fishing rod. I didn't have to sell my belongings to purchase a license. I paid as I went. Brooke was doing whatever it took to raise money to keep her drug appetite fed. My addiction was never a life or death situation. I kept my priorities in check and went when I could. Brooke's priority was her addiction.

I do, however, know of an instance where a man used his entire paycheck to support his gambling addiction. This man had a serious problem with poker machines, when they were legal. We had made plans on going fishing one night after we both got home from work, but we only made it as far as the local store's poker machine. With it being Friday and his payday, he was ready to play. I watched this man turn a $400.00 dollar paycheck into $1200.00 in winnings on the machine. He was excited, and I was ready to go catch a fish. He kept on playing and kept on losing. I witnessed him losing the $800.00 he had won, plus his original $400.00.

I didn't observe him having to go in and face his wife, knowing he had blown the rent money and grocery money for their two young daughters. I didn't have to listen to the fight that ensued that night. I did get to see the wonderful black eye and the stitches he had on his cheek from the brick thrown into his face. Then, I observed his wife and children leave him. After losing his family, he moved to Georgia, and I never heard from him again.

My entire outlook on life has taken a major directional change. Things that once bothered me, I let slide. Situations I felt were life and death at the time no longer worry me. I have learned not to sweat the small, and a lot of the big, things in life. Things once deemed as important are no longer a thought. As you are finding out, just like I did, through the loss of a child, there is nothing in the world that compares or matters as much as they did. The only thing that does matter to me now is taking care of my sons and granddaughter.

I will do everything within my power to help any alcoholic or addict I meet. I have learned that these people will not let everyone into their world. "If you can talk the talk, but can't walk the walk," they have no interest in speaking of their situation. I spoke with my friend about this very thing. I told him that with what I have been through with my daughter, I feel I am on the fast track to talk with anyone. He said, "Absolutely," and invited me to one of his recovery meetings. Before I was able to attend, he overdosed and passed away. This is four people I knew personally to leave this world from drugs in less than a year.

Not only do I want to talk, I want to help more. I recently attended some training offered by a local substance abuse group. I received training on how to administer Narcan®. Narcan® is the brand name of the medicine Naloxone®, which is used to counteract overdoses of opioids. I now carry 2 doses of the stuff with me at all times. It lasts about 15 minutes, while an overdose lasts much longer. But at least the 30 minutes time bought should be enough for the paramedics to arrive. It is like carrying a concealed weapon. I have it, I know how to use it, but hope I never have to.

The father part of me wants my baby back more than I

have wanted anything. But I would not want her back in the same situation she was in before leaving. She is free from pain, from worries, and free from drugs. Right now, I have one child who is completely safe. But I still have two sons and a granddaughter I have to worry about. I know I have done all I can do to raise my boys right, and now I can only pray. They have seen the devastation of drugs on this family, and, hopefully, this will be enough to sway them from going down that dead end road. I believe they will stay away from this horrible way of life, and death. But then, I also believed Brooke would stay away.

CHAPTER 12

In April, 2019, a benefit program was held to shed light on the addiction problem. It was a large show with over 500 people in attendance. A video which was previously made was shown, and I couldn't watch it. Others did and tears were flowing. People came up to me and hugged me. They all told me they were praying for my family.

The main reason for the program was to raise money to furnish bedrooms in a local recovery house. I was told it costs $5000.00 to furnish a room, and enough money was raised to furnish three rooms. About a week before the program, I found out that one of the rooms to be furnished would be done in honor of Brooke. Once completed, the room would be simply called "Brooke's Room." There will be a bronze plaque over the door with a picture of my baby hanging on the side. Women in recovery will be able to stay there while getting help from their situation. They will gaze upon pictures of past addicts who were not as lucky as they are to find sanctuary in such a caring place.

I am truly honored to think that someone would go to this length for Brooke. While standing on the stage as one of many parents who have lost a child this year, I was astonished by the number of parents standing beside me.

One thing I did notice was that there were over 50 people on stage, and I was the only father. We men do not like to be the center of attention, and I would have been just as happy sitting behind the curtain with no one noticing. I am by no means shy, but I don't like being in the spotlight. I also noticed there were several all over the room with napkins wiping tears. It was a solemn moment when we all broke our light sticks and held them high in honor of loved ones passed. I was truly humbled at such a scene.

I would like to mention my granddaughter, Baylee, had the opportunity to meet Miss Tennessee. This young lady was such an incredibly sweet person. She let Baylee and her cousin, Aybria, wear the crown she was wearing. This was the highlight of the evening for these youngsters. Since that night, Baylee has told everyone she knows she got to meet a "real live princess with a real live crown." She has no knowledge of the true meaning of the program, and was happy to just be there in all the excitement. Once again, the excitement and innocence of a child shines.

Since the benefit, I have been in stores on two different occasions when individuals would walk up to me and ask me if I was "that guy in the video." I would tell them yes, they would hug me or shake my hand, tell me how much that video touched them and they were praying for all families involved, and then walk away. These were total strangers that I will probably never see again. I am honored and touched in knowing people are watching it, and hopefully, it is making an impact on someone. The video has been on social media for about 5 months, and has had over 50,000 people view it. It is still going strong on the media and I pray it continues to touch lives and makes a difference in someone's life. If we can save one life, what we have done makes everything worth it. It is my sincere prayer that the words in the video fall upon ears who need it, and that lives are changed by it.

I have mentioned several times a program I attend that has literally saved my life. This program is called Celebrate Recovery, and it is phenomenal in helping those struggling, hurting, or just plain lost in life. I started going about two months after Brooke left, and I have been going every week since. It is helping me get my life back in order and my feet underneath me again. The aura of the entire meeting is like being with family. I never imagined being part of a family with over 300 brothers and sisters. It is truly overwhelming to walk in, be hugged, and be told I was loved by someone who was a total stranger a week ago.

Celebrate Recovery is a Church-based program started in 1991 in California. There are approximately 35,000 churches involved with the program. Countless lives have been changed through this program. It not only covers drug and alcohol addiction, but vast array of other topics. Compulsive behavior, anger management, sexual addiction, and mental issues are other topics. I am in a small group called "Family Support."

Family support is a co-ed group that deals with problems with addicted loved ones to child raising difficulties. It is a wonderful group full of caring people. Every group ends in prayer with a strong emphasis placed on our "Higher Power." I can honestly say I would have probably been gone if not for this program and my new family.

Some of the small groups are designated for men or women only. The reasoning behind this is that men are sometimes more comfortable to talk to men, and the same goes for women. The group I attend is co-ed. Family support covers topics that involve both mother and father. Young, old, or somewhere in the middle are invited to join a meeting any time. It is come as you are attire, and no one looks down on anyone for their life problems. It is a group of people from diverse walks of life, coming together and joining as one big family.

Every person at Celebrate Recovery is concerned with the welfare of other people. As my father once told me about teamwork, "There is no big "me" and little "you" there." Everyone is on an equal playing field. I highly encourage anyone with hurts or hang-ups to find a Celebrate Recovery program and visit it. Like I have stated before, it has literally saved my life.

There are things in this world we have no control over. We simply have to accept it and live with it. We have to understand drugs will always be prevalent, and drug addicts will continue to be created. This is a problem beyond our control and comprehension. As much as I would love it to happen, we can't terminate the influx of this problem without the serious intervention of government officials.

Just because one becomes an addict, doesn't mean the person is bad.

It simply means they have developed a problem that has a major hold on their lives and they need help. I am of the opinion that helping an addict is a better alternative than locking one up in jail.

Baylee, my 5 year old granddaughter's favorite saying is, "Suck it up, buttercup." This is not saying we have to suck up the pain of losing our child. We will live with the pain for the rest of our lives, and we won't be able to just suck it up. We have to find a way to deal with it. This part is what I, and every other grieving parent, deal with.

My feelings of "I want to show the world I am strong enough to take it and keep going as if nothing is wrong" is erroneous to say the least. Honestly, there is no one strong enough to take this pain and keep it tucked inside as if nothing is wrong. It will come out of each of us in one way or another.

We do have to suck up the fact that bad things sometimes happen to good people. We must understand that people come into our lives, and people go from our lives. This is just the way God intended. We must have peace of mind to acknowledge this. We must suck up the element that nothing is going to change what happened to our child. We must recognize the element that, eventually, death will visit and take us with it. There is no escaping death. As one man told me, "Regardless of what we do in life, we ain't gonna get out of here alive." How true this statement is.

There are, however, things in this world we do have control over. Things we do not have to accept and can change, if we have the desire to do so. Although we have to accept the loss of our child, we don't have to accept drugs as a way of life.

We have to accept that our lives will have an unrelenting longing for the precious life we lost. But, we can do things to help others and do what we can to make sure our child's death was not in vain.

Nothing can make our loss acceptable, but we can fight to keep other parents feeling what you and I go through daily. Avenues are abundant in working to help the struggling. A great way to help end this epidemic is to get involved anywhere possible. The more people spreading the word about this problem, the more light is shed on it.

This is an area where mothers excel. Mothers are masterminds at organizing movements and groups. When it comes to events, my hat comes off to the efforts of mothers. Many organizations have been developed by mothers and have gained worldwide attention. I am sure more organizations will be developed in the future, and I am sure fathers will be more than willing to help any way we can. God bless the mothers for what they do for the cause.

The Serenity Prayer is well known to many people. It is commonly used at AA and NA meetings. It is a simple prayer but full of profound significance. If you have never read or heard this beautiful prayer, I suggest you find a copy somewhere and memorize it. Local Narcotics Anonymous meetings are a great place to find a copy. It can be found on the internet. This prayer is great for alcoholics and drug addicts, but it is just as important to someone dealing with death of a loved one.

I recently found a roll of NA medallions in Brooke's personal belongings. I have no idea where they came from, nor do I truly want to know. I took four out of the roll and gave the rest to the Pastor at Celebrate Recovery. I was assured they would be put to good use.

The four medallions I kept were for me, Brandon and Cody, which we carry in our pockets daily. The 4th is put up for Baylee, and one day when she is old enough to understand, I will give the last one to her. With her being only 5-years-old when her mother left her, she has no understanding of what death is. She only knows that mommy and grams (her grandmother), are living with Jesus.

My mother and Baylee were always very close, but since losing her mother and grandmother, she has placed some distance between herself and my mother. She has developed a preconceived idea that love and death are tantamount with each other.

Not long ago, I asked her why she didn't like mamma anymore. She told me because mamma was old and was going to die soon. She has been hurt tremendously and is afraid of growing close to anyone for fear of death taking them. On the other hand, the relationship between her and I has grown very strong, just like her mother and I.

God bless the rational of our children.

Luke 18:16 says, "But Jesus called them unto him and said, suffer the little children to come unto me, and forbid them not: for such is the Kingdom of God."

The innocence of a child is truly remarkable. They trust everyone and believe whatever is told to them. They have no concept of right or wrong and must be taught. They see the world and all in it with eyes of purity.

It is our duty to raise our children as best we can. We are only stewards of God's property, and He expects us to take great measures in protecting His property.

Eight months after Brooke left, the same officer who initially told me about her passing came back to the house to bring her cell phone. They took her phone during the initial investigation. They were anticipating it holding a piece of key evidence, so they wanted to check it out. They were hoping to find the person responsible for selling the fentanyl-laced heroin.

When I opened the door and saw him, the feeling of the initial shock came back. For a moment, I was scared that something had happened to one of my sons. He saw the anxiety in my face and told me to breathe easy because nothing was wrong. The officer came in and we talked for about 30 minutes. He told me he was glad to see the progress I had made. I told him I was feeling better, but I had a very long way to go.

We spoke of the video a dear friend of mine had previously made. It was an interview of the two of us talking about the loss of our respective children. This officer explained it has forever changed his way of going about his job. He said he always saw the front of the scene, but the video showed him the back. It shows how parents have to deal with life after their loss.

His job was done when he told parents about their children. He never had to face those same parents again. He explained the video has caused him to become more compassionate and show better understanding to families he was dealing with. I was honored when he told me it was the deepest video he had ever seen on drugs and death.

The video he was referring to was the same one shown at the benefit program. My friend told me she was having it made for an event on how opioids hijack the brain. The video was made several months prior to the benefit show and put on social media. It was even put on the site belonging to the local sheriff's department. It has been described by many as the most powerful they have watched. I see it as nothing more than my sharing my feelings on film, and I was honored to be part of it.

The untitled presentation was made about four months after Brooke departed this life. I was not sure what I was in for, but the producer told me everything would be good. "Don't worry, be yourself, and tell your story," and "If you shed tears, it will be alright because people will be able to see your raw emotions." Within 3 minutes, the producer was crying her eyes out. I never intended to make anyone cry, but then I never wanted my baby gone either.

I wanted to tell my story, yet maintain my dignity. A man doesn't cry, especially in front of a camera producing a video for the world to see. When shooting began, I realized I didn't care if the world saw me cry or not. I was showing the world the pain that a parent goes through when dealing with death. The true pain goes deeper than what can be shared on video. It goes all the way to the soul.

I didn't plan on becoming popular, nor even want any attention focused on me. Instead, I wanted all attention focused on the message of the video. That message being that losing a child hurts intensely. It is on a social media site and has been viewed well over 50,000 times. As long as it is on media, this number will continue to grow. I hope it has helped in this struggle.

SIGNS TO WATCH FOR

Take care of your children, and watch for the telltale signs of drug abuse. There are signs every addict will display, so we must be prepared to pick up and act on them. Keep an open eye for such things as:

• **Mood Swings**: If your child is easy going and never temperamental, and all of a sudden he or she show signs of aggression, outbursts, becoming agitated at the least thing, and even shows changes in their personality, this needs to be addressed. Any dramatic changes in a person's personality are a sign that something is wrong.

• **Change in appearance**:   Things like a vivid loss of weight are a possible sign of addiction. So is loss of teeth, skin disorders, and even vision problems. Watch for any signs like these and be prepared to act. It could be the very action that will allow you to still have your child tomorrow.

• **Shirking of responsibilities**:   Job loss, repossessed car, eviction, inability to pay bills, and even lack of good judgment are also things to watch for. This was the sign Brooke displayed most. She lost her job and couldn't make good decisions. She didn't have to worry about her car being repossessed, as I was paying for it and all her bills.

There are many more indicators, but the main thing is to watch for things that are inconsistent with the normal way a child acts. Any abrupt change in character could mean something is not right. The biggest indicator I found was when things in my house started disappearing. I am talking about things of value that could be sold or pawned for easy money. One thing I am grateful to Brooke for is the things she took from me and pawned for low amounts of money. Guns and musical instruments she could have sold for several hundred dollars each were pawned for amounts of less than a hundred dollars. I don't understand why she let them go so cheap, but I thank her for doing it.

CHAPTER 13

Addiction can cause the best of people to lie to their families. The same people will become thieves and cheaters. They will do whatever they have to do to keep their demon fed. Think about the lies you have been told and things that have disappeared from your home. How about the late night phone calls from your child, asking if they could stay at their friend's house for the night? I remember the uneasy feelings of getting those calls. Is she really staying at her friend's house, or is she somewhere getting high?

Even after a year, every siren I hear still causes me to think they are coming to my house. It doesn't matter if it is police, ambulance, or fire, the sound of a siren still causes my heart to race and nerves to stand on edge. It has taken me almost as long to be able to pass a police car going in the opposite direction, and not thinking if it is headed to my house. I leave my phone in my truck when I work for fear of dropping it into some type machinery coolant or oil. When I come out and check for any missed calls, I am terrified when I see I missed a call from 1 or 2 members of my immediate family.

I would dial the number and first ask, "What is wrong?" I was always receiving calls from Brooke telling me she was going to jail, or Brandon telling me to be prepared when I got home, because the police were on their way out to pick her up. I have not had a call like that since she left, but I am still scared to answer the phone at times. It took some time before Brandon would say "Hello" to me. The first words from his mouth were "Nothing is wrong." This may sound crazy to some, but fear will linger more than one can comprehend. I know it has for me.

As hard as it was to acknowledge the fact that our child is gone, there is another fact that is just as hard to grasp. The other fact I am alluding to is that addiction kills people everywhere. It is as simple as that. This should be communicated anywhere we have the opportunity. If we could somehow get people to understand this single element, many lives would possibly be spared, and heartache would cease to be as prominent as it is. Addiction is not partial in who it takes out. It will take anyone who is available and willing it into their, soon to be, short lives.

Any person who sticks a needle in their arm, snorts, or swallows is a prime candidate for death. Although they get to a point where they no longer cared, our children really had no death wish, but that didn't matter. Once the choice was made, the outcome was already set in place. Life is short enough without making it needlessly shorter. Life is tough enough without people doing things to make it even tougher.

Other than the "Golden Rule" as mentioned in the 12-Step program earlier,

Luke 6:31 states, which I have applied to my life since youth, and I have lived with a motto of, "I don't care what you do at your house, as long as it doesn't affect me at my house."

Unfortunately, what happened to my baby, has indeed,

affected me at my house. Now the gloves are off, and I will do all I can to legally bring any dealer to justice. Not long after Brooke left, I was informed that her dealer was making deliveries to her at my home. What an uncomfortable feeling it is to know that someone like that knows where I live. I will unceasingly try to help anyone struggling as I may find. I have talked with many officers about helping and have made good friends with several of them.

I love the addict, yet hate the drug that made them. I have no problem praying for anyone and showing them love. I have no aversion in telling the world exactly how I feel about drugs or drug dealers. I have a sticker on the camper window of my truck, purely conveying my feelings. It has a simple message: "Shoot your local heroin dealer." Although I would never shoot anyone, I just want to share my distain for anyone making money from something that will kill our children.

I was recently stopped by a Deputy Sheriff for a non-working tail light. We talked for a minute and he told me to sit tight and he would be right back. Within a couple minutes, he came up and gave me a warning to get my light fixed. He then cracked a big smile and said, "I love your sticker." I proceeded to tell him about Brooke. I shook his hand, told him I appreciate what he is doing and I am praying for him, and then I left. I have had several officers, including the local Sheriff, tell me they love the sticker.

I am not saying we should become vigilantes on dealers, but I am saying we should talk with local law enforcement about ways we can help. Right after Brooke's passing, I spoke with several law enforcement agencies. I asked, and then begged, to be used in the fight against drugs. I was told by each one that I was too old and didn't fit the "profile" of a drug user. They told me I would only end up getting hurt. They explained the best thing I could do is be their "eyes and ears." This I can do and have done. We can all do more to help officials in the fight against drugs.

Here again, is another difference between a father and

mother dealing with the same loss of a child. I am not dismissing what anyone does to help in the struggle. The difference is that mothers tend to organize groups and help bring attention to the problem, which is wonderful. They work tirelessly to form groups to help others, and build lasting relationships between others suffering from losing a child or loved one. They work in putting together programs to help bring as much light to the situation as possible. I applaud all the effort going forth from mothers, because it was a mother that got me into such a group that protected my life.

Fathers, on the other hand, want to go for the jugular vein. The protector, provider, vindicator wants to get into the fight and eliminate the threat. This is understandable, but we, as fathers, must realize that we will quickly get in over our heads if our feelings are not curtailed. As much as we want to take the dealers on, we must let the police do their job. I have had to learn, just like any father, this is not our fight, regardless of feeling like it is. While it has affected our homes, we are innocent victims who can't afford to let our emotions get us into trouble.

I remember young men dating Brooke, and everything would be good, until one of them made her cry. Then, Daddy was ready to step in and do what was needed to right the wrong that had been done to my daughter. I have had her beg me not to do anything to them. The problem with me, and like most fathers I know, is we like to act first without looking at the consequences. A father has a more difficult time being compassionate than a mother. Compassion is usually not a strongpoint for men.

I remember telling Brooke's boyfriend and father of my granddaughter I had no problem with him dating her, but if he ever hurt her or made her cry, then he will have a problem with me, and that is really a problem he doesn't want. He treated her like a queen. Even after the two of them broke up, we have no problem with each other. We both realize it will take everyone involved to raise this child.

I have spent the last year of my life climbing out of a hole I was forcibly thrust into. While digging hand and foot holds, I reminisce about some of the advice I have gotten throughout this time: "Get up, shake the dust off, and put one foot in front of the other. None of us are promised a tomorrow, so we must make as much of today as we can. Our child is gone, but life goes on. The world does not stop for anyone. Play the hand you were dealt." Has anyone ever told you things like these? I have heard most of them from people.

I must say that after a year, all of this is pretty good advice. Every little bit of advice is correct, but it is not something a parent who has just lost a child wants to hear. They are words of attempted uplifting, and I can see these words being offered to parents, such as me. But, each one has a certain degree of indifference and indiscretion.

These words would come from people wanting to console, but not realizing what to say or how to say it. Each of these words of encouragement has been given to me by people. They are people who have never felt the harsh sting of losing a child, and would have difficulty in applying any of the comments to their lives. I know these individuals were speaking out of love, and I love them for trying.

I am a father, and I could not have applied any of these to my life a year ago. Then, I welcomed as much dust on me, covering me completely. The promise of no tomorrow was a welcome thought (almost a desire at times), and as for life going on, I was ready for mine to completely stop. I was ready to get off the ride and go home. Now, since the healing process began, I have learned that before giving any words of encouragement I weigh them carefully and pass them out, cautiously.

Time is all we, as parents, have to help in the grieving, longing for, and healing over our child. I have learned to spend my time observing and learning from others. I have always been a people person, and I find myself watching people anywhere I go. I love to go to the mall and sit down and watch people. It is amazing to watch total strangers with their children. I have seen actions ranging from almost child abuse to total neglect. It is sad to see a child acting like a little terror while the parents are oblivious to it and are lost in their own little world of shopping.

I appreciate observing elderly couples walking and talking together. It is evident they have been together for years and are still in love with each other. These people show what true caring for each other is. The man opens the door for the lady and she walks in. He will help her with things she is carrying. He will help her sit down before sitting himself. These are just good old fashioned manners that should still be used today. These people are beautiful to observe and, if given the chance, to talk with. They talk of when times were much easier, life was easier, and drugs were found only in hospitals.

I grew up in the country and loved going to our neighbor's house in the evenings. I was in high school, and I remember our neighbors talking about how things were when they were young. Our neighbors were both in their early 70's and could tell stories that would mesmerize me. I would sit on their front porch for hours listening to the tales of days gone by. Their world was nothing like our children's world.

Barn dances, and buggy rides were common occurrences in their youth. Men and boys would work in the fields, while the women and girls would cook, clean, and work the garden. I remember thinking how wonderful a life it sounds; no television, no telephone, and visiting a relative, or friend, over 10 miles away was a trip for the day. I have driven over 30 miles just to get something to eat and watch a movie.

House doors were left unlocked, and valuables were left in horse drawn buggies or cars with no worries of anything being stolen or even bothered. People were willing to help others because that was what neighbors were for. Not only were they willing to help, but they were ready to protect each other, if needed.   Doctors were not very close, and most of the elder women knew remedies for common ailments.   Not everyone had ulterior motives to better themselves by preying off others.   Happiness, love, and trust were the common denominator between whole communities.

The dances described sounded like something out of story books with very little to worry about.   There was always someone who brought some moonshine, and all the young men would slip out and get a little tipsy.   Everyone was happy and life was good.   There might be that one guy that like to fight and no one cared for him, but they still included him in events.   The only "drug" mentioned was when one man "drug" another one out to fight.   Sometimes, one had to be "drug" out of a hole his vehicle got stuck in.

The word "drug" is completely different in today's world. It means *a mind altering death trap*.   The legal drugs administered by physicians are not being questioned, but the illegal drugs are the ones taking lives.   Now, drugs are found everywhere and in every walk of life.   No one is immune and no one safe.   Drugs are turning up everywhere, and it is time for us to help stop it.

Needless deaths of our children are running rampant.   I am appalled at the number if recent deaths I am encountering, and the toll is rising.   Before Brooke's and her mother's incidents, overdose deaths were uncommon to me.   In fact, I knew of no one who had passed from an overdose.   Since then, I have been astounded by the people I have known personally to leave this world via the drug route.

Have you ever noticed that when you get a new car, you then observe all the same type cars on the road?   They were always there, but were unnoticed at the time.   These cars, same make, model, and even the same color as yours are seen all over the place.   The same is for addicts now.   Until I lost my baby, I never noticed any addicts around.   Like the cars, they were always there, just inconspicuous.   I am by no means saying the struggling are as plentiful as vehicles. I am saying as we learn their ways and mannerisms, the struggling are easier to pick out. If they are easier to see, it is easier to help them.

I visited another church today across town from where I usually go. I am usually out of church by noon, and this church doesn't start until afternoon. I was sitting on the back row, and the preacher was talking about a lady sitting directly in front of me. This lady recently lost her son due to an overdose. I felt like I was supposed to be there today. I spoke with her, as she looked through me with the same hollow eyes I once had. She listened to what I had to say, but am not sure if she even heard, or comprehended, my words. It is my sincere belief that God wanted me at that very place, at that precise time. I feel that He allowed me the knowledge to speak words she needed to hear. My prayers go to her and her family. This is another family destroyed by the enemy.

Seeing the raw grief in a parent's eyes serves to remind me how far I have come, yet how far I must still travel. I can talk about my baby for almost 10 minutes before my eyes become tearing filled. This is a major accomplishment, as I could not mention her name without going into convulsions. My dear friend lost her son four years ago, and is such an inspiration to me. I listen to the words she speaks, observe the things she does, and note the mannerisms in which they are done. Happiness overshadows any pain in her, but it is deep inside her. I only hope I am as strong as she is when Brooke's 4-year anniversary comes.

I am a member of several recovery groups on social media. There are always words of encouragement on these sights. I read stories of parents dealing with their addict child. I am in awe of how some of them handle situations. I have caught myself thinking. "What if I had tried that?" I listen to the words of recovering addicts and wonder in amazement the strength they must have. I realize they are fighting because their very life depends on victory.

In the world of the recovering addict, there is no second place. You either win, or you die.

I talk with many addicts and listen to the stories they share. It is horrifying to hear the things some of them have been through. Each recovering addict has my utmost respect.

Through my time of grieving and suffering stages, and working the 12-Step Program in my life, I have become aware that I am much more in tune with the feelings of others. I can, in a sense, feel when something is wrong in a person's life. I don't read minds, but have become quite astute a reading body language. I offer my help, making sure I don't push. If they want help, they get it, and if they don't want it, they don't get it.

As a concerned citizen of this great country, and as the father of a statistic, I have gotten involved in trying to get the attention of government officials. I have sent messages to local government agencies, to several state government representatives, and even to the President of the United States. I have yet to receive the first response from any of them. However, I do read that officials are beginning to realize that the opioid epidemic is out of control and needs to be addressed.

A friend of mine and I met with some local government administrators to discuss a proposal of developing some type of memorial for remembering our loved ones. Many of them are sympathetic to our plight. Ideas are still being developed in what we would like to do. Whatever is decided on, will be a memorial that is both beautiful and functional to the community.

I am not attempting to have attention thrown my way. I am happy to stay out of the light, just as long as something is being done. We are taking about some type memorial for all families of overdose children. Whether we want to admit it or not, it is a fact that every parent who has lost a child to drugs is held together by a common thread. Until this epidemic is brought under control, children and adults alike will continue to die from overdoses. We must all come together and fight to bring more light to this problem.

The meetings we had allowed us to realize most officials are eager to help with a memorial. They leave the choice up to us to decide. We were told when we have a plan and an area where to work, let them know. The memorial will be built sometime. As to when and where, that is still to be determined. I believe that the memorial will be beneficial in remembering loved ones, as well as bringing attention to the situation.

God never promised that everything in our lives would be perfect. He did, however, say He would see us through anything that comes our way. The death of a child creates unfathomable pain for parents. We love and nurture a child, do what we can to raise and protect that child, and then we are unwillingly forced to tell that child goodbye.

I am soon coming to the 1st anniversary of the passing of my daughter, Brooke. It is a day I am not looking forward to. During first few months, I found myself disoriented and unable to focus on menial tasks. The pain I felt was unbearable and unceasing. I have had a year to heal, and have come a long way, but know I have a long way to go. In my heart, I will celebrate her life, and the joy she brought me. I am sure feelings I once felt will resurface, and the pain will be real. I felt like I went through her death alone, but this time I know I will not be alone.

CHAPTER 14

The struggle that was within me, and caused me to question many things, up to and including the existence of God, is no longer relevant. The struggle is over, as I now have once again found my way. The pain will never leave and continue to let me know my daughter is gone. Yet, God is with me and continues to remind me that, while she is gone from my life, she is home and is safe.

She is waiting for all her family to once again, join and be with her forever. This gives me comfort and peace of mind as such that I can't describe. I will never again question Him or the choices He places before me. My God walks beside me every step I take. When I come to the point of no longer being able to walk, He carries me.

Psalms 23:4, "Yeah, thought I walk through the valley of the shadow of death, I will fear no evil: for thou art with me; thy rod and thy staff they comfort me."

There is no step I can take on Earth that God has not trod before. He knows the direction He is sending me and is preparing the way for me. I am *now stronger* mentally, physically, and spiritually than I was last year, as I was a total basket case then. I am not completely healed and realize I never will be. You must understand that healing will continue throughout your life.

I have been told all my life that every breath we take brings us closer to death. Well yes, it does, but also brings us one step closer to our complete healing. Every day, we struggle to make cognitive decisions concerning our lives and those around us.

These same decisions were not always easy to make, because our thought process was clouded. The more healing we gain, the easier things are to decide upon. Our complete healing will be when we are laid to rest. At the inception of this tragedy, I was ready for God to take me out of this world. Now, I understand that He has a purpose for me that I have yet to fulfill.

Unlike the feelings I had at the origination, I am glad God has kept me around. I am seeing things He has in store for me. Some things will be welcome opportunities; others will be not so welcome, or more difficult to do. But, if God places them before me, I will heed His will, and do my best. When my job is complete here, God will call me home, and I will happily go.

By enduring the torment placed before me, I have learned to lean on my Higher Power. Through all the loss, depression, hatred, anger, denial, and all else I have faced, He has given me strength and grace to overcome it all. There were times felt I walked alone because my eyes were blinded by emotions.

After enduring times when I thought God cared not, it was when I realized He was closer to me than ever. Each parent, both mother and father, will realize eventually that our Heavenly Father is closer to us than we are to Him. He is there when we need Him and will never force Himself upon anyone.

I am a man, a father, and I am flesh and bone. I have feelings and I have a certain amount of pride. I am not prideful by any stretch of the imagination. But, I am proud of my accomplishments and my children. I helped bring three wonderful children into this world and did my utmost to be there for them and protect them. I tried with everything I had inside to raise them right.

I have two children living, and one child waiting for me at Home. The pain of losing and the longing to see my daughter can't outweigh my responsibilities to my others. I have had to learn how to keep my hurt subdued, while being attentive to my sons and granddaughter. It is a chore to learn to juggle feelings, but we will be forced to learn.

Never let the hurt you feel overflow and cause your other children to suffer. Our children are suffering from the loss of their sibling and need us desperately.

Keeping the feelings over my daughter reserved does not mean I miss her less. I miss her as much today as I did the day she left. I have just learned to keep them under my control. I think about her daily, but I have learned that I can no longer let thoughts of her consume me. My sons are grown with lives of their own, and my granddaughter takes a great deal of my time, but it is time well spent.

Just like with Brooke, I have become Baylee's rock and her safety. I have an enormous fear of failing her, but I then realize I didn't fail her mother. I was not invited to share the part of her life that involved using drugs. That part of her live was reserved only for Brooke and her mother. I simply didn't recognize the few signs of needing help that she was showing.

Baylee wants to learn to play piano and sing like her mother. I told her when she gets a little older, I will get her piano lessons. There is so much I want to teach her, and tell her about her mother, but right now, it will just go over her head. I have to wait until God shows me the right time. It is painful when she asks, "What happened to mommy?"

How do I tell a child her mother passed away from an overdose of an illegal substance? I have to bite my tongue and tell her that her mommy was sick and she took some medicine that worked the wrong way. Right now, that is enough for her. What I tell her is not stretching the truth, nor is it a flat out lie. Her mother had the disease of addiction, and the medicine of heroin worked against her. I have to tell her the same things about her "grams" (her grandmother).

I love my granddaughter dearly and will do anything I can for her. When she gets older, I will endeavor to keep from enabling her. But, if and when she falls, it is my hope to be there and help her up. I will give her room to grow and make her own mistakes, like I tried to do with Brooke. I hope she learns from her mistakes better than her mother did. My prayer for her is that she is able to keep God first in her life.

Even though her father has custody of her, he has allowed me to take her to church every time I go, which is every time the door is open. I want to make sure she knows who God is. She loves going to Sunday school with me. She sits beside me when I am in front of the church playing my guitar. Timid and shy she will never be. She has already decided that in time, she will be playing piano and singing in church just like her mommy did.

It has become a Sunday Morning ritual for us to get a sausage and egg biscuit on the way to church. She is now pushing the envelope by asking about that biscuit on Sunday night and Wednesday night. I tell her they don't have biscuits at 7:00 PM in the evening, and she will tell me it is ok, she will just "take a cheeseburger."

I pray she finds a good, young man that will honor and cherish her. May she find happiness in her adult life because her young life has been filled with sorrow. I do everything I can to keep that precious child smiling and laughing. My boys are still my world, but this precious little angel from God, is my life.

Wish me luck as I am planning on teaching Baylee how to fish sometime in the next few months. The only time I took her mother fishing, she came very close to sticking a hook into my hand. I yelled out, and she cried from knowing she almost hurt Daddy. I tried to console her and tell her it was an accident, and that I actually didn't get stuck with the hook.

She was 7 at the time, and it was the last time she picked up a fishing pole. She would camp, and build fires, but never again went fishing. Brooke was always a Daddy's girl with a tom-boy outlook. Since I couldn't take her camping with the Scouts, her brothers and I would go camping with her. She could put up a tent, build a fire, cook over the fire, and loved it.

When she grew a little older, she gave it all up to become more involved in church. Her decision of getting involved in music and children's choir thrilled me immensely. But, she still loved to build fires and toast marshmallows.

The last time Brooke was with us toasting marshmallows was about a year before she left this world. She helped me build a fire in the pit and as we were getting ready to start toasting, she told me she needed to go to her friend's house quickly to get Baylee's jacket that she had forgotten. There was a little nip in the air that night, so I didn't think much about it. She was gone for 1 hour, 2 hours, and then 3 hours, so I called her. I received no answer so I called her brother, Cody. He told me someone had Brooke's phone and was making calls trying to find family.

The lady with Brooke's phone told Cody she had overdosed and passed out while in my truck. She passed out while driving my truck and was at a total stop in the middle of the road. Brooke fell over in the seat, with the truck running. The truck was still in gear and the motor was running with Brooke's foot still on the gas pedal. By a total miracle from God, my truck was at a complete stop. It should have been moving, but it wasn't. The first people on the scene were an off-duty paramedic and his wife. They were going out to eat, when they approached the truck from behind. He got out and immediately started working on Brooke while waiting for the ambulance. I was later told she was barely breathing and was a bluish-gray color. She was rushed to a local hospital and was given a dose of Narcan®.

The blood work came back from the laboratory and showed Brooke had fentanyl in her system then. Had it not been for the actions of the paramedic, Brooke would have surely died then. Her life was spared that night. I asked her the next time I saw her, how many chances does God need to give her before she got the message. Each time, she told me that was her final message, and that time scared her enough to straighten up. I heard that so much over the next year, that I quit asking. God gave her chances for an entire year, but it went unnoticed.

Brooke was a beautiful, living, breathing creature that was placed in my life by God. She laughed, cried, sang, and got extremely mad, because she was human. She was much more than simple statistic on a state information board. Your child was the same. The only way we will see our child again while on Earth is through a photo. It is not fair, neither is it just, to be forced to carry all the memories of how they were. It is all in combination of what we gave up when we lost them.

What would Brooke have become? Would she have become the nurse she talked about becoming? Would she have been married? How many more children would she have had? How many of her songs would have been recorded and published by her? These are questions that will never be answered. I know there was nothing more I could have done for her, but there was so much more that she could have done for herself.

I remember her as a child talking about what she wanted to do when she grew up. Like most young girls, she wanted to be a teacher. As she grew older, she decided she wanted to be a nurse and work with children. She would have been incredible in that role. She always had an affinity for young children. She tried several times to develop a children's choir in church, but found it to be difficult with only four small children there. She then decided to just work on a quartet. That worked out better for a while.

When she became a young adult, her desire was to marry a preacher and help in his ministry. She always had a passion to be around children. There is so much potential wasted in every child. Each of my children is totally different with completely opposite personalities, so I have no idea what was lost when she left this world.

Psalm 91:2 tells that, "He is my refuge and my fortress; my God in Him I will trust."

We do not know the reasoning behind anything God does in our lives. It is not for to know, nor is it for us to question. I have learned that whatever God does in my life, I will trust Him completely. For in Him I find shelter from the dark forces of this world. When this world comes against us, we can stand and fight or give it to God.

Every time I stand and fight, I loose, but when I give it to God, I come out victorious. This world came against us when things took our children. We will never have them back, but if we rely on God and His mercies, He will see us through the toughest of storms. Many battles have been won by people willing to get on their knees.

My friends are, and always have been, here for me to talk with. I share some of my burdens and concerns with them. They help me with what they can. When I am alone and scared in the darkest of nights, I can call on my God, and he can relieve me of all my problems, not just some. God is truly my refuge and my strength. He will be for you during this terrible time in life.

As a father, I need not to be pitied. Please understand the statement, as I mean no harm. I do not need for anyone to feel sorry for me, nor treat me as an invalid. I have regained my strength, and have had time for my mind to refocus on life.

I am healthier, both mentally and physically, more now than I have been in quite a long time. I do, however, appreciate all the words of comfort given me throughout this entire ordeal. I know that many prayers have gone up on behalf of my family and me. I know that prayers are still going up for us.

Prayers are going up for you and every other parent dealing with the loss of a loved one. It is my hope that the pain and suffering we have dealt with, to be overcome by His glory and grace.

What I went through, and am still dealing with, was an atrocious occurrence. But my baby is gone and nothing will change that. I face each day with emptiness in my soul and am learning to deal with it. Dealing with it on a daily basis makes it easier, but it is something I wish to never forget. If I forget the sharp sting of the pain I feel, then I will grow complacent and perhaps unable to help others.

Dear God, please never let me forget the pain I have endured. Let me use it as a weapon of war to fight against what took my child from me.

It is our responsibilities as parents, to do what we can to protect our children. Sometimes our children will stray, and sometimes they may become the victims of circumstance. Brooke became a victim of circumstance in her addiction.

If we do all we can to provide for our children, and strive to be good parents teaching right from wrong, and the child goes astray, is it our failure? How can it be? We can't be around our children 24 hours a day and protect them from life. We simply do the best we can and pray it is enough.

The influence this world places on young minds is powerful. Sometimes it is powerful enough to sway the strongest.

Matthew 7:1-2 tells, "Judge not that ye be not judged. For with judgment ye judge, ye shall be judged: and with what measure ye mete, it shall be measured to you again."

Before this heartbreak with Brooke took place, I knew no drug addict personally. I will admit that I had somewhat of a predisposition against them. I saw how television shows made them out to be, and I believed it. To me, an addict was some type of draft dodging, hippie, freak type person. These lowlife individuals would steal, rob, hurt people and do what they needed to get their drugs. I had a mindset that all drug addicts should be locked up, never to be let out into society again. To me, they were worthless pieces of garbage that should die from their addictions. I had this biased notion throughout my young life, and most of my adult life. My mind was made up long before I met one.

It is with a very heavy heart and total embarrassment that I must admit, I was wrong. May God forgive me for the predisposition in my way of thinking. It is sad to think it took my daughter becoming addicted and passing, for me to realize that addicts are only people with a serious problem. They are people just like you and me.

CHAPTER 15

Drug addicts, alcoholics, and those addicted to anything else, are people like you and me. The choices made that placed them where they are in life, were not always theirs to make. Before becoming addicted, these people were valued individuals. Like us, they had families, jobs, outside interests, and cared for others. When misfortune befell them, they became outcasts to society.

Many were shunned and ridiculed for their problems. They were told, "You would be alright if you just stopped taking, or drinking, that stuff." It is not as easy as that. The blame was put on them for their inability to stop using. The blame should not always be put on the individual.

It is not our assignment to judge each other. We were not placed on this earth to pass judgment, but to help anyone when the opportunity arises. I am by no means saying we should open our doors and invite an addict in. It would be extremely difficult to invite an addict into my home and trust that person. It was a difficult experience that I could not trust Brooke, my own flesh and blood, in my home. I am saying we should open our hearts and offer our support.

All we can do for the struggling is to offer help. The choice is theirs to either accept the help or not. Addicts do not care about themselves, because no one else cares for them. They have given up on life because society has given up on them. Society has had the concept that is easier to lock them up instead of helping them. It is a slow process, but people are beginning to realize it is more beneficial to help an addict recover than to incarcerate them.

Long ago, I heard a prayer about not judging someone until we walk a mile in their shoes. I will be the first to admit that my outlook on someone struggling would be quite altered if I were in their place. My attitude would be totally different. I recognize it took the death of Brooke for me to see this and adjust my mentality toward addicts.

I think my problem stems from being a man who was unwilling to change my attitude. I am a man who has led an unwavering life. I would see people as I wanted to see them, and not as they actually were. The solution to my way of discerning was when I saw my daughter become a person I no longer knew.

I have other ideas about the drug dealers. These are the people making money from the suffering of our children. I think these should be the ones put away for life. Unfortunately, there are more of our children dying from drugs than dealers being found. Once again, the father's philosophy comes out in me. My mind was telling me, the need to protect my children outweighs my need to act realistically.

I needed to become the animal willing to do whatever it takes to protect my young. My heart was telling me to think things over before acting. This is a dangerous predicament to be in, as a judgmental spirit will rise and take away some of the peace we have worked so hard to rebuild. A man can get into much trouble thinking with his head and not his heart.

I have learned to give this type temperament to God, and

ask Him for guidance. Many times I could have ended up in jail for what I wanted to do. It took prayer and reading God's word to overcome my old way of thinking. Nothing I know of is worth going to jail over. As hard as it was to see Brooke through that partition, I imagine it would be even more distressing looking through it from the other side. I don't look good in stripes either.

When I was a younger man, I was with friends, riding back from a place we should have never been in the first place. It was a bar and we had been in there having a few drinks and shooting pool. We were much younger and there was nothing else close enough for us to do. After finishing our game, we decided to go to another friend's house and hang out.

As soon as we pulled out of the parking lot, we saw blue lights fall in behind us. My friend tried outrunning the car that was now chasing us. He didn't make it far before wrecking his van. We were alright, but got to spend the night in the county jail. I am not telling this to brag, but quite the opposite. There are happenings in our lives that shame us, and this event is one such happening in mine. We spent only 24 hours before being bonded out. I was never as proud of freedom as I was then.

I can't imagine what Brooke went through during her 90 day sentence. It is inconceivable to even fathom a longer period of being locked up. Those 24 hours were enough for me to realize jail is not a good place to be. I have yet to be in another situation where I was on the wrong side of the police. I will do anything to prevent me spending another night locked up. Had I not used restraint concerning the situation Brooke forced upon me, I would have been locked up for a very long period. This would have been totally unacceptable to me.

Once someone is locked up and forgotten for the duration of their sentence, there are very few opportunities to improve one's self in a county jail. Prisons, on the other hand, do offer types of rehabilitation. If one is unfortunate enough to have not graduated, some prisons offer help in obtaining certificates of graduation. They offer rehab programs to make ready a person to be re-introduced to society. In some instances, drug rehab is available in a lot of prisons. If one does go to prison, as Brooke almost had to, a person can go in addicted and come out recovering. I am not saying it is a good thing in going to prison. I am saying it is better to do to what one must to avoid going there. If Brooke had gone to prison for stealing the rings, she would still be there, possibly be getting help for her problem. But she didn't go, and she isn't here.

In my past, I have known many men who spent time in prison. They told me stories of goings on in the "Big House." Just listening and never being there was enough for me. Some of the men I knew completely turned their lives around. One is now a preacher. One of the men I was acquainted with came out and was back in within a month. Nothing in his life changed before or after. A very dear friend of my parents was a preacher before going in. He did some dastardly acts that got him arrested. He was serving his sentence on death row. He never saw freedom again, because after serving about four years, he hanged himself in the shower.

Watching Brooke live with addiction showed me she was in a different type of prison. It was a prison within her. The mannerism of the self-induced sentence she was serving was just like what my friend described. Inmates were to do as they were told, and if they got out of line for any reason, they would pay the penalty. Drugs made her do what she was told, because they were the warden of her life. They dictated her life in every way imaginable. They told her when to sleep and when to wake.

If more was needed, the drugs would order her to get money however she had to and buy more. If she didn't do what she was ordered, she paid dearly. The drugs imprisoned her, controlled her, and discarded her. They gave her the ultimate death sentence to be carried out immediately. Drugs are unforgiving and unrelenting in their quest to control people.

I became aware I was in a type of prison myself. I was reluctantly dealing with something I was never prepared to handle. This hellish nightmare I was thrust into was my warden. I could sleep or eat only when I was allowed. I couldn't enjoy things I did, because it was not in the warden's best interest. I was forced to stay as compliant as possible to prevent waves. My mind was told what to do, and how to act. None of this was directly caused by my own doing. None the less, I was here dealing with my sentence, just as Brooke had to deal with her own.

Brooke paid the price of death for her lifestyle. I know your child did, too, and for that, I am truly sorry for your loss. We are left behind to pick up the shattered pieces of our life and move forward. All the pieces will never be arranged as they were before, and some will never be found, but we must keep trudging on. My trek seemed like a mountain with sheer cliffs I had to climb. I thought I would never make it to the peak. After a year of trying and suffering many setbacks, I can see I am nearing the top. I am anxious to see to discover the view that lies ahead of me. I am anxious to discover what God will be doing with me over the next horizon.

I am realizing that with all I have dealt with over the last year, I am no better, but also, no worse than I was then. I am still a man and father trying to find his way in doing what is best for my remaining children. I have also found that no matter what has been hurled my way that my God is still God, and my God is always good. Last year, I would have argued with someone on that point. Many prayers have gone up on my behalf, and are going up on your behalf.

I recently had the opportunity to speak with a lady fresh from losing her son. I saw my grief and pain in her eyes, and understood that I must use what knowledge I have gained to help her. I spoke words of comfort to her, and told her I knew her pain, because I share it with her. She looked at me with the same hollow look I gave to many, as I told her she would smile again. She looked trustingly into my eyes and I knew she heard what I told her. I am telling you, my unknown friend, you will again smile. Life will grow around us and we will take part in it. Just like the oyster, we will coat our pain and suffering with prayer, and will go forward helping others.

My fatherly outlook of vindication has ceased, and my future is full of hope. It is not a hope for myself, but a hope that I can be used to help in this fight.

My family has stood behind me and encouraged me to transcribe this book. It has not been the easiest project I have undertaken, but it has helped my healing process. I pray it has touched you while reading it. I have prayed for God to give me words of comfort to whoever is reading it. It is amazing how much healing I have received by simply putting words on paper. I have read and re-read every word I have written and gain new strength each time.

I will suggest to you, that even if you never intend on writing a book, to consider writing a personal journal. Innermost thoughts, feelings, pains, questions can be scribed, without fear of condemnation from anyone. They are your thoughts and are for no one except you. You may never want to read it again, but something as simple as writing your outlooks can help your restoration. If you have never written before, you are not alone.

I hated writing essays in high school, and college term papers were worse. I started simply writing notes and thoughts to myself. I had sticky notes all over my house and in my truck. I thought I needed to write them down so I could remember them. Before I realized it, I had about 30 pages of notes. I took the notes and started organizing them and before long, I was writing this book.

I once worked with a man who lost his wife. She was a delightful lady, and he had every reason to be proud of her. She had cancer and passed away within a year of discovery.

He was devastated and had no idea how he was going to survive. He found a group and shared his feelings with, and it was helping immensely. He did something he heard from another in the group. He wrote a beautiful letter to his deceased wife, describing in detail how much he loved her, and how much he was missing her. He wrote a very intimate letter describing everything he wanted her to know. It started out as a letter, and then turned into a pamphlet, then a small book.

I was allowed to see the book, but was never allowed to read any entry, which was fine. It was completely personal and between him and his wife only. He wrote about 60 pages to her, and then took it outside and burnt it. This sounds crazy, but it truly helped him. I think it was more the writing his thoughts than burning it that helped. Either way, he was able to find the peace that we all seek.

As an option, if you keep your thoughts written somewhere, you might decide to share it with someone new to the club. Your words might explain the feelings they are experiencing. The clarification of feelings were once felt by you, might be enough to let them know they will make survive their ordeal. This is exactly why I am writing this book. I know by writing it, I hope to help others with the words contained herein. Whether it does or not, it is helping me by being able to read what my heart is allowing me to put to paper.

We are all human and the feelings we have of losing our child will be unique to each, but in many ways, will be exactly the same for us all. In listening to many people talk about their loss, I have heard my feelings coming from other mouths of people suffering the same hurt as me. When we finally get to a point of helping others, we will see many similarities in what is being shared and what we felt. Don't be shocked to hear this, as we will be able to relate and be more able to share our feelings.

Recently, I was given the opportunity to give my testimony at my Celebrate Recovery meeting. I take this as a huge honor and am totally scared to death about it. Although I have spoken in public, I am not a public speaker. I am doing this because I believe it is what I am expected to do. People need to know the struggles of a father in times of distress. I believe that God is going to use the words I speak to touch someone.

I am not doing this for my glory, but for His. In all things I do, I want to give my God the glory for helping me survive through this trial. I told the representative over the CR program how petrified I was, and he told me he would be worried if I was not scared. I pray my story will be such that I will be invited to visit other groups and share my story. I will go where ever God leads me to go and share.

Last year, I didn't want to speak to anyone about my suffering, and now I am ready to share it with the world. Until now, I have not shared my inner feelings of this incident with anyone. I realize it is time for the world to know what this father has dealt with. I hope it can help others in dealing with the same devastation happening around them.

The suffering that each one of us deals with, I liken to an oyster developing a pearl. Sand gets inside the shell of an oyster and becomes an irritant. A liquid is applied by the oyster to the sand to keep the irritation down and the liquid hardens. As the irritation returns, more liquid is applied. This is repeated every time the sand starts irritating again. The liquid hardens and a pearl if formed. When the pearl of a salt water oyster is harvested, the oyster usually dies. The sand inside us is the pain we feel. We coat it with whatever we can to keep the pain from irritating. When the pain returns, we repeat coating it with anything that is helping us heal, like helping others. When our pain is finally over, it is because we have rejoined the one in which we were hurting over.

Now I understand we are more than oysters, but they have an innate defensive weapon to avoid irritation inside the body, and we do as well. They use a hardening liquid to coat the irritant, and continue to do so until the irritant is removed or the oyster dies. We have weapons we can use to coat the irritation inside our bodies. We use things like prayer, talking, and helping others.

We all have an inherent coping mechanism within us. No matter what life throws at us, we can handle it if we step back, truly observe the situation, and find avenues to work through it. This mechanism is called strength. It has been said that God will never put more on us than we can handle. I was starting to doubt that, as I knew I could never handle what was on my plate. Through much time, prayer, talking, and helping, I found I could handle this situation. It took great strength to conquer such pain which I am still working on, but in the end, I am still here.

1 Peter 5:10 says, "And after you have suffered a little while, the God of all grace, who has called you to his eternal glory in Christ, will himself restore, confirm, strengthen, and establish you."

This is simply telling me, and I hope it tells you, "Relax and breathe easy, God's got this under control." Just like an addict starting in recovery, we can overcome our situation by growing closer to God and allowing Him to take care of it. If we try to gain victory over this fight within ourselves, without God, we will lose. We will lose much more than we are willing to give up. This is not a battle for a little piece of ground, but rather a fight to the death.

Giving our problems to God is a simple thing to do. Not picking them back up after giving them to Him is more difficult. We must learn how to do it. Many times I have given my problems to God, only to pick them back up. We must learn to lay our problems of God's feet, walk away, and never look back. Who takes the trash to the outside can, and then goes out and brings it back in? The words "Faith and Trust" were used earlier in this book, and they are going to be used again.

We have to come to an understanding that our trust in God becomes imperative. We have to learn to trust Him to take care of us in our time of need. Then, the word "Faith" comes in to play. After learning how to trust God to see us through, it is significant to have the faith that He will do it.

At the onset of my trials, my trust in God was severely tried. I started to doubt His very existence. I found myself wondering if God knew my name or if He even cared. I fought with this way of thinking until I got back into church and Celebrate Recovery. I soon found God to still be very much alive and waiting for the chance to help me recover my ability to function. Celebrate Recovery, along with getting back into church, allowed me to see God never left my side. When times in my life grew despairing, He carried me through the rough waters and placed my feet firmly upon solid ground.

I remember thinking to myself. "Lord, I am not going to make it. I feel like I am about to die. The pain is too much for me to take." I felt this way for quite some time and soon realized, little by little, I was going to make it. The saying, "That which does not kill us, tends to make us stronger," is in my case a very true statement. In time, it will be true for your situation. The loss of my baby didn't kill me and has only intensified the strength and determination of fighting this outrageous epidemic. I could not have stood as tall as I am now, and not as tall as I will be in the future.

I am a year older since Brooke left. I am more willing to share my side of what I went through. I share because I want to help others. I care nothing about honor, fame, or being in any spotlight. Seeing others succeed is honor enough for me. I have been this way all my life. Any Scout from our troop that earned his Eagle rank was the only award I needed. The smile on his face and gleam in his eyes produced a smile in my soul that will be with me forever. I have helped those stranded with a flat tire by changing it for them. I never once took money, and I barely exchanged names with them. I receive a wonderful feeling of joy when I can do something to help improve someone's life.

Throughout this entire book, I have tried to convey my feelings and sentiment of the loss of my daughter. I have attempted to show how a father will grieve and suffer. No two fathers are alike and will suffer differently. We will all go through every stage of grief at our own pace. I am simply trying to shed some light on the differences of how a father grieves. I take nothing away from the grieving of a mother. The mother is usually the first to come to the point of healing. It is not because mothers love less, nor suffer less. They become more willing to show their openness in talking about things and starting the healing process sooner. The beautiful way mothers come together and help each other is amazing to say the least. Yet, we men, the lone wolves, try to work things out on our own.

Throughout the lives of all my children, not just Brooke, I have achieved a vast amount of memories I will cherish forever. I have attempted to share some occurrences and recollections upon these pages. Some things written in this book have never before been shared. It is difficult for a father to share parts of his life with anyone. We don't like letting others into our private space. It isn't manly to shed tears or talk about heartbreaking events. I am way beyond caring who sees me cry. My child is gone, and the amount of tears I have shed in public would fill a swimming pool. Any pride I had within myself has been discarded, and I no longer care.

The pride I had, almost cost my life. While younger, I was always too proud to ask anyone for help. Nothing was so hard I couldn't handle it on my own. I didn't want to talk about my problems. I was in charge of how I handled things around me.

Proverbs 16:18 says, "Pride goeth before destruction, and a haughty spirit before a fall."

My way of thinking as an ordinary man and father came very close to taking more than I was willing to give. I had to clean up a lot of messes I made and ask forgiveness from my Higher Power and those around me.

I have written many pages of grief, suffering, longing and healing, but I have yet to write about closure. In my heart I see no closure to this horrible incident. Sure, Brooke is gone forever, and the history of her precious life is closed, but her memory will abound always. As long as we have the memories and talk about our child, they are still around.

Brooke lives in my heart and the hearts of her entire family, because we refuse to let her memory go. It is testament to her life from her friends sharing the love they had for her and the love she shared with them. Her life was full of love for God and helping others. Many of her friends tell me how she helped them in their struggles. I know Brooke would have been pleased to know that many of her friends have adopted me as their father figure. I have been told she always talked about me and what a good father I was. Several of them, now my other daughters, have told me they wish they had a father like she did.

In Brooke's eyes, I was some type of a superman or some fictional beyond belief father. In my eyes, I was just a father doing his best to take care of his children. I loved them as much as I knew how, and did my utmost to show them every day. I know she loved me, but I am just now beginning to see the depths of how she needed and depended on me from her friends.

Each of us know how much we love our child, and one day we will find how much our child loved us. Words may not come from the child, but friends who were confided in with their innermost secrets. We may find out immediately, or it might take a year or longer. I am still finding out things Brooke said about me to her confidants. Her best friend once told me, "You have no clue how much she loves you and how much she needs you." I thought I knew how much, but I realize I didn't see the "me" she portrayed to others. It, somehow, makes me feel closer to her when I hear her friends talk about her. I know she lives in their hearts as much as she does in mine.

Our grief will subside, and our pain and longing will become a way of life. The memory of our child will never fade but will be somewhat overcast with new burdens of life. The healing will continue as long as we breathe, but none of it will ever be fully closed.

Our complete and total closure will be when we close our eyes to this world and join our child and other family members waiting for us in that other room. While we live, we will never have a complete closure due to the number of unanswered questions we have. The only one who can answer the questions to satisfaction is gone.

Upon examination of the differences in how mothers and fathers handle loss, I have to say both are as strong as the other. There is a vast difference in behavior between the two when dealing with the loss of a child. I am not saying either side is right, while the other is wrong. There is no wrong way for a parent to grieve and handle the hurt. Mothers work with other mothers, and the healing process begins much sooner than for fathers.

They are more willing to talk their struggles through and listen to each other. Mothers shed tears easier than fathers. Fathers definitely shed tears, but in the privacy of their own space. We do not want people to think we are not men when we cry. Real men cry and are not ashamed of who knows it. I have cried at church, at the store, and even in my small group meeting. No one made fun of me, and everyone understood.

It is no question in knowing the unspeakable pain a mother goes through during childbirth. During the first months, there are many sleepless nights due to baby crying, baby hungry, changing baby. A responsible father will share the nightly duties of taking care of baby. I helped all I could and was happy to do it. Since Brooke left, I have relived every step of her childhood.

I remember bringing her home from the hospital all the way to remembering her first day of school. Those five years seemed to rush by so quickly. I remember changing Brooke's diaper one day, and the next, she was introducing me to my granddaughter. Where did the time go? I saw her Baptized and survived her memorial service in the same church. The pain of losing a child is a different type of pain as childbirth, but it is just as unspeakable. It is a pain both parents share.

I was allowed to witness her being ushered into this world, and I was there to grieve her leaving. I remember a wise man once saying that when we leave this world, the marker on our grave will show the date of birth and the date of death.

These dates will be separated by a simple dash. The year of birth or death is nowhere as important as the little dash, as it is a testament to our life. The dash on my baby's certificate shows her love for all mankind and willingness to make things better for all concerned. It is full of love and laughter with a side dish of crying and praying for others.

Think about the dash on your child's marker. Let that dash remind you of the joy and happiness that child had. Let it be a memorial to the love of God and family. We all need to let that lowly little dash symbolize all the good things in our child's lives, and know there was more good than bad.

My baby has been gone one year, and my life has been a total nightmare. Her passing seems like it was yesterday, but also feels a thousand years ago. At one time, I was a father intent on doing whatever was needed to take care of those hurting my children. It was difficult to allow anyone into my world of grief and pain.

Now, only a short year later, I am the same father, but with a new outlook on life. I no longer hate the world. Depression and anger that once kept me down no longer consume me. The hurt and longing is still there, but covered by love of helping others. My life is as whole as it will ever be.

My daughter is at rest in the arms of God. She hurts no more and is safe from anything desiring to do harm to her. She is happy and waiting for her family to come home.

I now start a new chapter of my life, dedicated to helping the struggling. I hope that within the pages of my writings, I have shown things to allow you to ...

See it from my side...

ABOUT THE AUTHOR

Mark Timothy Webb was born September 26, 1959, in Knoxville, Tennessee, and raised in southern part of Middle Tennessee. He graduated Loretto High School in Lawrence County in 1977 before attending Maryville College in Blount County, Tennessee, for a short time.

Tim is a loving and caring father of three children: Brandon, Brooke, and Cody. He is also "Papaw" to his only granddaughter, Baylee. He spent 14 years serving in leadership positions with the Boy Scouts and Cub Scouts with a long tenure as Scoutmaster and Committee Chairman of BSA Troop 1804. For the past 10 years he has been associated with Freemasonry, serving in several officer positions, and is a 3rd Degree Master Mason.

He is an avid outdoorsman that loves hunting, fishing, and camping in the natural world that God has given to us to enjoy and admire His works. Tim is totally at home in the outdoors. He also plays bass guitar, and as a man of God, has played for several churches and Gospel groups for years.

Tim loves life and is willing to help anyone at any time. He has an affinity for putting others before himself. After a 25-year career assisting and caring for oxygen patients in the home healthcare industry, Tim is now a strong advocate in the war against drug abuse. With same caring heart, he currently assists others in the drug recovery process and gives public awareness interviews and presentations concerning his daughter, her death from opioid addiction, and the dangers associated with improper drug use and abuse.

Tim is a member of several real world advocacy, recovery, and social media groups focused against drug abuse.

TWO ARE BETTER THAN ONE

Ecclesiastes 4:9-12 "Two are better off than one, because together they can work more effectively. If one of them falls down, the other one can help him up. But, if someone is alone, there is no one to help him... Two men can resist an attack that would defeat one man alone."

Celebrate Recovery is a Christ-centered, 12 step recovery program for anyone struggling with hurt, pain or addiction of any kind. Celebrate Recovery is a safe place to find community and freedom from the issues that are controlling our life. It is not just for those with drug-related issues, but for all affected by the drug crisis. Locate a Celebrate Recovery Group near you and learn about the many programs offered to assist you and your family. Many people share your experiences and concerns. Seek them out. You will be glad you did!

Learn More Today
celebraterecovery.com

**Ask, and it shall be
given you;
Seek, and ye shall find;
Knock, and the door shall
be opened unto you.**

Matthew 7:7

NOTES, QUESTIONS & NEW FRIENDS MADE

NOTES, QUESTIONS & NEW FRIENDS MADE

NOTES, QUESTIONS & NEW FRIENDS MADE

NOTES, QUESTIONS & NEW FRIENDS MADE

Made in the USA
Monee, IL
30 March 2020